Seeking Your Loved One
on the Other Side

"Matthew McKay, a grounded man with a scientific orientation, was unexpectedly transported into an alternate reality cracked open from the passing of his beloved son, Jordan. This tragedy acted as a catalyst, thrusting him into a sphere of experience he had never anticipated. During Matthew's metamorphosis, he came to understand the continuity of consciousness after physical death and the possibility of communication between realms. He also learned to appreciate the subtle nature of such communication, which required him to tone down skepticism and 'trust that feeling.' His insights are a gift to us all, especially those who have suffered the pain of losing a loved one."

MARK IRELAND, AUTHOR OF *THE PERSISTENCE OF THE SOUL*

"Matthew McKay's story of seeking and finding Jordan after death is a masterpiece of psychic detective work, clairvoyance, personal faith, and cosmology that brings the living and the dead into alignment."

RICHARD GROSSINGER, AUTHOR OF
BOTTOMING OUT THE UNIVERSE
AND *HOMEOPATHY AS ENERGY MEDICINE*

"Matthew McKay's *Seeking Your Loved One on the Other Side* chronicles a father's pilgrimage from the devastating loss of his son, Jordan, to the discovery of the eternal nature of the soul. Through the use of hypnosis, journaling, and spirit communication, McKay's book provides a lighthouse, offering hope and guidance for those navigating grief. This book is a testament to the strength of the human spirit and the enduring bond between worlds."

AUSTYN WELLS, AUTHOR, SPIRITUAL MEDIUM,
AND SOUL GARDENER

Seeking Your Loved One on the Other Side

Communications with the Invisible Universe

A Sacred Planet Book

MATTHEW McKAY, PH.D.

Park Street Press

Rochester, Vermont

Park Street Press
One Park Street
Rochester, Vermont 05767
www.ParkStPress.com

Text stock is SFI certified

Park Street Press is a division of Inner Traditions International

Sacred Planet Books are curated by Richard Grossinger, Inner Traditions editorial board member and cofounder and former publisher of North Atlantic Books. The Sacred Planet collection, published under the umbrella of the Inner Traditions family of imprints, includes works on the themes of consciousness, cosmology, alternative medicine, dreams, climate, permaculture, alchemy, shamanic studies, oracles, astrology, crystals, hyperobjects, locutions, and subtle bodies.

Cataloging-in-Publication Data for this title is available from the Library of Congress

ISBN 979-8-88850-233-4 (print)
ISBN 979-8-88850-234-1 (ebook)

Printed and bound in the United States by Lake Book Manufacturing, LLC
The text stock is SFI certified. The Sustainable Forestry Initiative® program promotes sustainable forest management.

10 9 8 7 6 5 4 3 2 1

Text design and layout by Tona Pearce Myers and Debbie Glogover
This book was typeset in Garamond Premier Pro with Avenir LT Std, Gill Sans MT Pro, and Soleil used as display typefaces

To send correspondence to the author of this book, mail a first-class letter to the author c/o Inner Traditions, One Park Street, Rochester, VT 05767, and we will forward the communication, or contact the author directly at **SeekingJordan.com**.

Scan the QR code and save 25% at InnerTraditions.com. Browse over 2,000 titles on spirituality, the occult, ancient mysteries, new science, holistic health, and natural medicine.

To Jude—
for what we were
and what we have become

Contents

FOREWORD

by Ralph Metzner, Ph.D.

THE TRAGIC AND VIOLENT DEATH of Matthew McKay's son sent him on a turbulent intellectual and emotional pilgrimage to discover the meaning and truth of our existence. Matt, a professional psychologist and educator committed to the materialist paradigm at the core of the modern social sciences, consulted me because he knew of the death of my eight-year-old son in a bicycle accident forty years ago. The death of a child is such a violent rupture in the normally anticipated cycles of life that most people, including professional psychologists, are stunned into incomprehension. This book is the account of Matt's mythic journey to reconnect with the immortal soul of his beloved son and reestablish the connection that had been ruptured by Jordan's early and violent death.

Not only did Matt, in time, make a conscious connection with Jordan's soul, which has given him great personal solace, but he has gone further and established an ongoing conversation with Jordan. As a committed radical empiricist in the tradition of William James, Matt recorded the visions, dreams, and communications he received from his son. This approach allows the received insights and teachings to be considered, reflected, confirmed, or modified by other observations. This book is a first expression of this project shared between incarnate father and discarnate son. Matt states, "before any of this was written, Jordan outlined the entire book. During a session of channeled writing, he named each chapter and described its contents. It took five minutes."

Matt adopted my suggestion of setting aside a special time and place in his house to regularly sit to commune and communicate with Jordan, writing down the impressions and communications he received. As with all observations, the ones we make about the nature of life beyond death are subject to confirmation, extension, and modification through repeated questioning and the observations of others. It turned out that Matt, a trained hypnotherapist himself, could very easily enter a conscious trance state from which he could later remember everything that transpired. This book contains a record of some of our sessions, as well as completely independent observations by Matt, channeled communications from psychics and mediums, and the observations of other individuals who have known Matt, Jordan, and their family.

Matthew and Jude McKay and their family were friends of my family. My stepson, Eli Jacobson, Jordan, and their friend Chris formed a trio of adventurous teen-agers in their last two years at Berkeley High School. Our families would see each other at social gatherings. The teens and their respective friends would cluster in small circles among the larger groups of adults. Like all teens, they had their own way of telegraphing shared interests and observations. In the writing of this foreword, I wanted to complement Matt's observations of Jordan's after-death journey with some memories Eli had of his friend in this life. This is what he wrote:

I met Jordan on the first day of my junior year of high school, introduced by a mutual friend. After a few weeks of school, maybe around the time of the 9/11 event, we really started to gel and hang out. During that year, some of the people from our group went to a rave in Oakland. That was my first time doing Ecstasy. Jordan was there, but he was not interested in doing drugs, except for occasionally smoking pot. He came along and took care of the rest of us.

During our senior year, our most common weekday activity was meeting at a café in Berkeley to do home-work together. It was usually an after-dinner meeting from 7 or 8 PM until the café closed at 10 or 11. These study sessions were not all that productive as far as schoolwork goes. Jordan actually seemed to enjoy help-ing us with our homework more than he liked doing his own. If Chris or I were ever stumped looking for a topic to write a paper about, or if we needed an outline and couldn't get it started, Jordan would take over and get us going. He was really smart and very capable of succeeding at anything he was interested in.

Jordan was always interested in money. Those nights in the café, he would sometimes bring the *Wall Street Journal* and read it while we were hanging out. He would keep track of stock quotes even though he didn't have any money invested. He had a dream of being rich, and he was studying the stock market to get a feel for how it worked so he could take advantage of it someday when he had enough money to really get into it. He and I had a little business in high school: we would buy candy bars at Costco and sell them to other students for a decent profit. We didn't make a lot of money, but enough for lunch on some days, and we had fun doing it.

Jordan also loved music. He played the guitar and was always interested in getting the highest-quality sound he could for listening to music or watching movies. He had these incredible speakers in his room and had invested quite a bit of money in a special amplifier and high-quality headphones for his iPod.

Jordan had a great sense of humor, and he would keep everyone in any group laughing constantly. That said, his humor was not for those who were easily offended. Nothing was off limits. In every picture I have of Jordan, he is either smiling or making a ridiculous face.

One curious thing about the story of Jordan being shot is that he had a history of being a target. I really don't know what to make of this, but in high school on several occasions he ran into trouble and would get beaten up. Chris and I never had that problem. Maybe it was because we were bigger, or perhaps it was just chance. Jordan wasn't particularly small, and he was feisty and would fight back if someone was attacking him. One time, he went into a bathroom and some kids followed him in and tried to beat him up. He was able to shove them out of the way and ran out, but he was a little shaken up by it. Of course, these kinds of things weren't unheard of at Berkeley High. I just think it's interesting that he was targeted those times in high school, and then again that terrible night in San Francisco that ended his life.

When he sent me that story, Eli knew nothing of the connections and insights related in this book. But his comment about Jordan being caught in violent confrontations with others is consonant with the account Matt writes about a violence-prone past life Jordan had as a bootlegger in the Prohibition era: "Because of these activities, he lived in fear of the police. . . . Jordan then sought balance in his next incarnation (his life with us). Though he feared anger and had a phobia of the police, he found safety in his life with us. . . . Three times in his life as Jordan, he was a victim of violence—and karmic forces, unknowable to me, were at work on the night he died."

This book documents the paradigm-expanding journey of a psychotherapist and social scientist led by his own experience to recognize the reality of a multidimensional universe. I see a parallel between this book and *Proof of Heaven*, in which neurosurgeon Eben Alexander describes a near-death experience. Alexander is a recognized and influential authority in his field of medicine, as Matt is in the social and psychological sciences. Their accounts of the reality of individual lives and consciousness beyond the veils of mortality are important expressions of the expanded worldview that our society needs and is moving toward.

Many of us understand and can verify through our own experience that it is possible to communicate with our relatives who now exist only in the nonmaterial spirit world. But this does not invalidate our observations of ordinary reality. Rather, it expands and enhances them with unsuspected depths of meaning and beauty.

Seeking Your Loved One on the Other Side intersperses descriptions of Matt's meetings with individuals who knew Jordan, sharing memories and post-death visions, with his reflections on their meaning and with channeled statements by Jordan. If Jordan's statements seem to reflect a wisdom far beyond that of someone his age, it is because he is no longer subject to the limitations of Earth-centered knowledge and can access the multidimensional universe in all its depth and scope.

In response to his father's question about purpose, Jordan's soul-spirit tells him, "the purpose of matter— whether in the form of circling planets or the human body—is to help consciousness grow. All of physical existence serves this purpose. Consciousness creates matter and the laws of the universe. Then it manipulates and lives in physical worlds in order to learn and evolve. So *every* event is an opportunity for souls to grow." This is truly a book to be read and contemplated, offering both solace and wise inspiration.

RALPH METZNER, PH.D. (1936–2019), was a clinical psychologist; professor emeritus at the California Institute of Integral Studies in San Francisco, where he taught for thirty years; and founder-president of the Green Earth Foundation. His books include *Maps of Consciousness*, *The Unfolding Self*, *The Well of Remembrance*, *Green Psychology*, *Overtones and Undercurrents*, and *The Life Cycle of the Human Soul*.

"the bird lies still while the light
goes on flying"
—W. S. MERWIN,
FROM "UNKNOWN AGE"

PREFACE

We are here—each of us—for a reason. And the pain we face—each of us on this planet—comes for a reason.

Pain is the path to truth. It refracts light to reveal things not otherwise seen. In the heart of pain is a moment when the universe, and our place within it, becomes more visible. This is a story of entering that moment, of listening to what pain teaches.

Six years ago, I lost something more precious than my own life. At that moment, I began the journey you'll find in this book. I wanted to know the truth about why we are here and what happens after death. So far I have learned this: Nothing is truly lost. Nothing. The soul is constant, never broken. Pain seems to damage us, but the damage is an illusion. The idea of safety or protection is an illusion. It is *all* safe—everything we love.

This is the story of how I came to know these things. I am not a psychic or a medium; I am not clairaudient.

I am, rather, a psychologist with a deep love of science. I am a researcher who conducts randomized, controlled trials. I'd never expected to take this journey. But as I have learned, in the heart of pain exist things I'd never imagined.

CHAPTER 1

Train to Chicago

Sunrise touches the Utah mesas, lighting high orange cliffs above the gray chaparral. The train sways through the curves and switches. Rio Grande coal cars fill a long railroad siding, ending at the broken windows of the Desert Moon Hotel.

Jordan is dead, killed by men who wanted something. Either his possessions or simply the pleasure of inflicting pain. If they hoped to find power by creating suffering, they have succeeded. By putting a bullet in his back, they took our son, and so much of what made life mean anything to us.

As the early light works through the crevices and canyons, we are on our way to Chicago to meet a man who has found a way for the living and the dead to talk. His name is Allan Botkin, and he knows how to induce a state in which those who grieve can hear directly from the ones they have lost. I don't fully believe, but it's all I have.

Jude and I sit on the edge of our narrow bunk. We

have pictures and mementos of Jordan's life. The light is stronger now, the world outside the window no longer hidden in shadows. At this moment, our journey feels absurd. The clarity of light suggests the eternal separation of what can be seen from what cannot, of the physical and known from the hoped for and ephemeral.

Jordan's ashes are in the closet of his room back in Berkeley. They weigh about the same as he did when I first carried him from the nursery to his mother. And now we are trying to find him, to reach past every empty place to hear his voice again.

In Chicago it is gray, with wind careening off the Great Lakes. Allan Botkin practices, weekends only, in the office building of some large corporation. We meet with him in a conference room situated within a rabbit warren of work cubicles.

Botkin explains that the procedure he uses for Induced After-Death Communication (IADC) was discovered by accident. As a psychologist with the Veterans Administration (VA), he often treated post-traumatic stress disorder with core-focused EMDR, Botkin's own variant of eye movement desensitization and reprocessing (EMDR), developed by Francine Shapiro. It's a simple process that encourages patients to visualize a traumatic scene and then move their eyes back and forth. The eye movement serially stimulates opposite sides of the brain, inducing a gradual reduction of emotional pain. A large body of scientific literature documents the effectiveness of EMDR; it works with about 75 percent of trauma patients. I am a psychologist. I have used EMDR myself, hundreds of times, primarily with people suffering the effects of early sexual abuse.

Botkin stumbled into his Induced After-Death Communication protocol with Sam, a veteran who had never recovered from the death of Le, a young Vietnamese girl he had planned to adopt. Botkin guided Sam through numerous sets of eye movements as the man focused his attention on his sadness and on the memory of Le lying dead in his arms. When Sam reported that the pain began to subside, Botkin did one more set of eye movements but with no specific instructions. Sam closed his eyes and fell silent. Then he began to cry. When Botkin prompted the man to describe his experience, he said, "I saw Le as a beautiful woman with long black hair. She was in a white gown surrounded by radiant light. She thanked me for taking care of her before she died. . . . Le said, 'I love you, Sam.'"*

Botkin realized he had witnessed what might be an after-death communication—made possible by a simple variant on the EMDR procedure. He set out to discover if Sam's experience was replicable. Over the next several years, Botkin initiated the new procedure with

---

*Allan Botkin, *Induced After Death Communication* (Charlottesville, VA: Hampton Roads, 2005), 11.

eighty-three patients at the VA. All were suffering profound grief. None were told what to expect, other than a general description of EMDR and its effectiveness with trauma and grief. Eighty-one out of those eighty-three patients experienced an after-death communication—98 percent.

Once Jude and I are settled in the conference room, Botkin interviews us together. Later, we each come alone for the EMDR procedure. When it is my turn, I notice that Botkin's face seems etched with some residual of the pain he's witnessed. He moves slowly, as if his limbs carry an invisible weight. To guide the eye movement, he uses a wand made from a thin PVC pipe edged in blue tape. "It works," he says, beginning a steady movement of the wand.

He asks me to imagine the scene in which I learned of Jordan's death. It began with a call from the San Francisco medical examiner. "I have the worst news anyone can get," the man said. "Your son was riding home on his bike late last night—around one thirty—and he was attacked on the street. He was shot. I'm sorry to say he died at the scene."

And then I had to make my own phone calls. "We lost Jordan," I would say after apologizing for having sad news. At the time, the meaning of the words had hardly sunk in, but as I sit with Botkin they burn like acid, and I can barely stand to think of them.

During the EMDR, I focus on the sound of the words:

"the worst news . . . we lost Jordan." Over and over, my eyes follow the wand moving. I see Jordan slumping in the doorway where he died. Botkin continues until an odd numbness sets in, a lifting of the weight.

This is the way EMDR works. I have seen it so many times with my own patients—how they begin to let go of the pain, how the frozen images and feelings start to soften.

"Close your eyes," Botkin finally intones. "Let whatever happens happen."

Nothing. A distant panic starts—that I have come all this way for silence. That my beautiful boy is unreachable; I will never hear from him again. I wonder if the fact that I use EMDR in my own work, and know what to expect, is getting in the way.

I open my eyes. Then Botkin moves the wand once more and I follow it. Again he enjoins me to close my eyes, to let go to whatever happens.

And now, quite suddenly, I hear a voice. Jordan is speaking, as if he were in the room. He says:

Dad . . . Dad . . . Dad . . . Dad. Tell Mom I'm here. Don't cry . . . it's okay, it's okay. Mom, I'm all right, I'm here with you. Tell her I'm okay, fine. I love you guys.

Those are the exact words. And they convey the two things I most needed to know: that Jordan still exists and that he is happy. The pain of his last moments is long over, and he is in a place that feels good.

The next day we leave Chicago. Jude, despite all our hope, hasn't heard Jordan's voice. For her, the silence of the dead remains. All I can give her are words that only I heard. But I feel a sense of reconnection. What had been severed is again whole; what had been lost has been given back to me. I heard my boy. I learned that on different sides of the curtain of death we still have each other.

On the train home I feel lighter. But as we cross the gray waters of the Mississippi, I have a familiar thought: that Jordan can't see this, that all I experience—and all I feel—is unknowable to him. I touch the window as if reaching for something. Then I remember his words: "I'm here with you." Moments later, light fades on the old brick facades of Burlington. I imagine showing it to Jordan.

CHAPTER 2

Beginning the Conversation

WHEN WE CAME HOME, Jude and I resolved to listen and look for Jordan in any way we could. I wrote in my journal:

> The left hand doesn't know the right hand. The conscious mind doesn't remember what the unconscious holds. All around, the voices of the dead are speaking. But we are afraid because it's considered madness to listen.
>
> On the right side of the brain we can listen—because that's where we intuit; that's where we know wisdom. On the left side, we make up the story of being alone. Invisible.
>
> Our hands join in prayer. But the prayer is speaking without listening. The mind finds words for love. Describing it. Seeking the beauty of being known, accepted. But we remain deaf to the chorus that bathes us. Holds us. Takes each step with us.

Time moves us downstream from each loss. The living relationship is further away, left on the bank where we last embraced, where the last words were spoken. Across that distance stretches silence, the helplessness of what can't be fixed or undone.

The last time I saw Jordan was at lunch at Saul's, a deli he was fond of. I can't remember what we spoke of. He was doing well—a job he liked, a lovely young woman he'd recently moved in with. I do remember the corner where I hugged him goodbye, feeling his thick, wiry hair against my cheek, his strong arms around me. I said, "I love you," as I had thousands of times, and then I began half-running to my car, late for something.

I had no inkling this was the moment we were leaving each other, and that every moment since would bear me further from his arms, his eyes, his sweetness. It was so ordinary, so embedded in our daily lives, that it held no portents of loss. And when I look back, I feel as if we are still there, still hugging on that corner. I can feel him holding me, and sometimes I can believe the embrace still exists—that I can have it, reenter it anytime I want.

But time moves us downriver. I craved more than memory, more than the few words I'd heard in Chicago. I wanted a two-way conversation, like we'd had at the deli.

I wanted to ask questions and hear answers. I wanted to know my boy again.

In hopes of having that conversation, I consulted Ralph Metzner, a psychologist who has learned the art of channeled writing—an ancient technique for reaching across the divide of death and communicating to souls in the spirit world. Ralph himself lost a son, and he spent years searching for ways to reach him.

There was another connection: Jordan and Ralph's stepson, Eli, had been best friends. I knew instinctively that anyone I connected to through Jordan could be trusted. And Ralph had known Jordan well.

———

His office is set up in the former dining room of an old Victorian. High mahogany wainscoting reaches to a shelf near the ceiling; there is a crystal chandelier. Ralph, a thin man with wispy white hair and eyes that have a wounded look, explains the process so I can learn the steps and do it at home. Channeled writing works best when it is done in the same place with a set ritual. It helps to have an object that connects you to the dead, and it is also beneficial to first engage in a practice that helps you enter a receptive state. Breathing meditations work well, as do candles for focusing attention.

"How will I know I'm not making it up?" I ask him.

"You can't escape uncertainty," Ralph replies. "There

will always be doubt. Just listen to Jordan; see what he says. Your feelings about it will guide you."

———

I have a desk that my parents gave me when I was eleven. Whenever I sit at it, I feel how objects connect us to people who are gone, and sometimes to an earlier version of ourselves. I sat here as a child, doing homework, distracting myself with small toys, and looking into the enticing darkness of my backyard.

Now I sit here alone, assembling objects: A cobalt blue glass mask, with a lit candle behind it, that my daughter, Bekah, brought from Mexico. And a blue business card Jordan created while he was in high school. It reads, JORDAN MCKAY, CEO, OMEGA TECHNOLOGIES. There was no Omega Technologies, but it got him into countless trade shows for Apple and other technology giants.

I begin with my breath, counting the exhalations till I reach ten, then starting over. I focus on my diaphragm, the genesis and center of the breath. Some spiritual traditions recognize this spot as the locus of "wise mind," where we can access the deepest truth of our lives. When thoughts arise, I notice and label them—"There's a thought"—and return attention to my breath. After a while my mind settles, and a calm begins that touches every part of my body.

I suddenly wonder if this is some kind of hokum I've

fallen prey to. Then I worry that I haven't done it right, that I haven't prepared sufficiently to hear Jordan's words. "There's a thought . . . and another thought."

I stare at the flickering candle behind the mask. I imagine that it is Jordan's presence, like the sanctuary light in the Catholic churches of my childhood. And now my mind begins to quiet again. I open my notebook and write the most urgent question: *Are you happy?*

The answer is instantaneous; it arrives before I've finished the question. It comes in the form of a whispered thought, with the timbre and pitch of Jordan's voice. I write:

More than you can know.

Then I write more questions and record the answers.

Do you miss me? I have you with me.

What are you doing? Studying. Learning things. Getting ready for what I have to do next time.

Next time? I'll be back soon. I want to help the planet. Last time I wasn't going to have time to do anything, so I practiced focusing my will, finding beauty.

How can I connect to you? Watch for me when I come to you. Watch the signs. Feel me inside. Trust that feeling when you sense I'm with you. The circle stays strong with love. Just remember your love for me. Open the channel so you can hear—just like you're doing now. This is the circle, letting me through. I love you, Dad. That's how it is. I'm right with you. I'm here with you and Mom. Just feel it. It's real. My arms are around you. Always.

What is the circle? The practice of love keeps the circle. It's like a discipline. Practicing love isn't collecting sad memories. It's feeling the whole person, without thought, without judgment. It's holding all of them at once.

The circle is all of us, living and dead. All connected, all talking to each other. It's no different now than when we talked at Saul's. Our relationship is the same, Dad.

I'm exhausted; I blow out the candle. I want to believe everything I've heard, but I hate self-deception. It's a response I inherited from my father, a man who despised the ways people lie to themselves to justify their needs and actions. But suddenly it's clear: I will have to live with that remembered contempt in order to keep listening. If I want to open the channel so my boy can talk to me, then I'll also have to live with doubt, perhaps even ridicule.

———

I have had more than a hundred conversations with Jordan since that first time. I share his answers to my questions with Jude, who, with the assistance of the spiritual medium Austyn Wells, eventually found a way to receive his answers to questions of her own.

The relief of feeling Jordan on the other side—answering me—has been enormous. Yet so has the doubt, the sense that I am violating all my commitments to science and reason. To ease my misgivings, I asked Jordan why anyone should do this. What can be gained and lost? His immediate answer was that *nothing* is lost by opening to the circle with the dead. Nothing. But here is what such conversations can gain us.

- First, and most important, we preserve a connection across the life-and-death divide; we break the silence.
- Next, we are able to receive support from the dead. We know we are not alone here without their love and counsel.
- We also can learn things that only the dead—liberated from the amnesia of physical life—can know. This includes knowledge about life purpose (why we have come here) as well as information about what happens to the soul after death.
- We can find greater acceptance for the pain in life. The conversations with Jordan have provided me with a long view of the cycle of life and death, a sense that death is a minor transition that doesn't change soul relationships.

- Finally, such conversations allow us to give support to the ones on the other side. We can hold and love each other, knowing that the embrace never ends. I believe that Jordan can feel my love as an active intention and that it strengthens him.

The meaning of our last words, that last touch outside of Saul's, has changed for me. This is how Jordan put it in a recent conversation:

> There will never be a last thing we say to each other. We have been learning from each other for centuries. We have been guiding each other across many lives. Why would we stop when we hugged each other goodbye on Shattuck Avenue? Dad, we will never stop loving and learning. I promise.
>
> This is part of what we came here for—to learn to reach across. To not succumb to this deafness, the shouting behind glass. We can hear each other across the barrier. We have learned the art of telepathy, of talking without mouths and ears. Telepathy and trust are how the living and the dead converse. That's all channeled writing is: telepathy.

Jordan mentions other lives, which we'll explore in detail later. For now, I want to emphasize one thing: Telepathy across the barrier of life and death is possible. In fact, it is easy. I have no special powers. I am not clairvoyant or clairaudient. I do not see dead people. I am not privy to the future. Rather, I have merely learned to listen—using ritual and focused attention—to my boy.

CHAPTER 3

Listening

IN THE SILENCE, as we wait to rejoin each other, as we touch reverently the objects that connect us to the dead, something is born. What we knew as truth together must be found again—changed by listening in the bitter quiet.

The ones on the other side wait for us to listen, for the moment we are ready. They will come then in dreams, in the feeling of a presence. They will come as animals or in passing murmurs on the street. In the high mountains they'll come as streams or granite.

We make pictures of angels—tall, with alabaster wings. We have given them roles: the angel of death, the angel at the gate. But in truth the souls who have passed from this world are like us—survivors of life and death.

In the ways we seek to be heard, they seek to be heard. In the ways we watch helplessly while people we love dissolve and collapse, they watch us struggle, consumed by the illusion that we are alone.

The angels, the people we love but cannot see, try to

reach us. Within the first year or two after their death, they often direct an outpouring of communication to friends, family, present and past relationships, even distant acquaintances—anyone who is receptive and able to receive the message. Such dreams, feelings, or whispered thoughts are often answers to questions. And if the person who needs the answer can't hear it, usually someone else will.

In the silence after Jordan's death we sought his spirit, trying to feel his presence in his room or in nature. We waited for dreams and looked for signs in some unusual occurrence. Nothing. We could feel only our own pain; we could hear only the quiet of the house after the mourners left. It remained for others—perhaps no less heartbroken, yet more receptive—to make early contact with him. We encouraged them to write down their experiences, and the messages started immediately.

At 2:00 AM on September 17—the exact moment Jordan died—Mauchi, his employer and friend, awoke with a strong sense of Jordan's presence in the room. He had no idea what it meant because he didn't yet know that Jordan was dead. The next night Eli, Jordan's friend, awakened to what he thought was an earthquake. The shaking was so intense that he rose and stumbled to the floor. Suddenly he felt Jordan's presence. He later said that it was as if the room had filled with Jordan's essence, with pure love.

Four days later Elena, a friend of Jordan's older sister, had this experience: "This morning I awoke and Jordan was there. What I got was that he is in a state of pure contentment. He is unadulterated love. He is not in pain or chaos or sadness. His life has been completed. He may have been surprised by the turn of destiny, but he is at peace."

But he did have unfinished business. When Jordan was killed, he was on his way home to the flat he shared with his girlfriend, Elisa. "I keep getting the vision of him being an arrow stopped physically in midflight," Elena wrote to Elisa. "The night of Jordan's death he continued on his path home. He feels a responsibility toward you. He was careful to convey that he has deep faith in your ability to recover. I think Jordan very much saw his home as the home you have together. He loved the space you created. He very much saw himself making a life with you."

The message went on to request that Elisa keep a colored stone in memory of him. Elena's note continued: "He urged me to go to your house, and I did, and I understood. When I entered your room, I was drawn to a happy window ledge filled with brightly colored rocks and shells. There was one stone in particular that most closely resembles the stone that came to mind first. That is the one that is enclosed [with this letter]." As it turned out, it was a stone that Jordan and Elisa had found together. "Know always—as was made very clear—that he will carry a piece of your heart with him, and you will carry his heart with you."

Jordan was making sure that the people he loved were hearing from him.

Ten days after Jordan's death, my friend David Feldman had a dream. He described it to us in a letter:

> The dream appears as an animated painting. On one side, in somber tones, Jude and I are standing together in grief. We are looking away from Jordan, who is on the other side of the painting. He appears in manga style—bright colors, happy, dancing. He is trying to get our attention, dancing around, but we are preoccupied with our pain and don't see him. Jordan is happy, even ecstatic, and wants us to know he's okay. The dream is a message. Meant particularly, I think, for his mother, Jude.

While Jude was grateful to hear of David's dream, she struggled with the pain of hearing nothing from Jordan herself. At about this time, Elena received another message from Jordan. This one was directed to his younger sister, Bekah. "He stated that he has grown up with Bekah and that his spirit will speak through her children. And they will be protected by him."

It was unclear what this meant—whether he expected to reincarnate as her child or would simply watch over

Bekah and her offspring. A later dream, experienced by my friend Catherine, clarified the meaning. "In the dream, Bekah was traveling a great distance, and Jordan could be seen flying directly above her—in the form of an angel. He looked exactly like the angel in Chagall's *Lovers in Moonlight*. He was protecting her."

On some level Bekah got the message, because a short time later—without ever hearing about Catherine's dream—she gave us a reproduction of *Lovers in Moonlight*.

Within the first few months after his death, Jordan appeared in dreams to each of his close friends. Always he laughed and joked, assuring them he was still around, still with them. But there was one dear friend—Chris Houston—who received no initial contact from Jordan. Perhaps, Chris suspected, it was because he was a skeptic who didn't believe in an afterlife. Nonetheless, months later, Jordan eventually made contact. Chris dreamed that he and Jordan met in San Francisco. They went walking, engaged in a long conversation. Eventually they arrived at a café, where Chris took his leave.

In the dream, Chris walked on alone. He later told me:

I very clearly remember thinking to myself, "This can't just have happened; Jordan has passed away." I remember feeling very uncomfortable, as if my unwillingness to accept Jordan's death was finally catching up to me, and I was losing my mind. I quickly turned around and headed back to the café. As I entered, I once again saw Jordan's face. With a feeling of rising insanity, I asked Jordan if I could speak to him again. We walked outside, and I admitted that I felt I was going insane—because there was no way we were having this conversation, as he had died some months back.

At this moment I realized I was dreaming and said as much to Jordan. He ignored my dreaming comment, but went on to tell me it didn't matter that he'd passed away; it didn't make our conversation or time together any less important or real. Because he was still very much alive inside me.

Chris's dream had a vividness he wasn't used to. "This dream somehow felt much more real than almost any dream I'd had before. But this concept is hard for me to understand and accept, as I'm a very skeptical person."

There are dreams and then, I suspect, there are visitations that take the form of dreams. This kind of vivid, "realer than life" dream is reported by many who've had a loved one die. The dreams feel different because they include the true psychic presence of the one who was lost. They also differ from normal dreams because they frequently contain a direct message—specific information or instructions delivered from the dead to the living. Chris's dream is an example of these visitation experiences, not just in its unusual vividness but also in the clear message:

their conversation was still *real* and Jordan was still present despite the fact that he'd passed away.

Hearing of these dreams and encounters with Jordan gave me comfort. He was finding open channels and seeking the people who could receive his voice. The ones who were dense with pain, or who sought contact without having anything to say, often ended up waiting. Communication across the barrier between life and death is not very different from other forms of discourse: you have to listen to hear anything, and you have to have a clear, coherent message to be heard on the other side.

In the days after Jordan's death, I was almost *demanding* contact. I sought him with a fierce determination that muddied rather than cleared the channel. His efforts to reach me collided with my cacophony of emotions, which rendered me psychically deaf, even while my only conscious intention was to listen.

Over time I began to let go. Not of Jordan, but of some expectation of what I needed him to say. As the shark attack of grief turned more into a deep yearning, dreams began to come. The first one included a dear friend who had died. Peter, my old partner at the Haight Ashbury Psychological Services, was holding a child version of Jordan in his arms— with the clear message that my boy was being cared for by ones who loved him on the other side.

Then came a dream in which I was lifting Jordan's spirit out of his lifeless body. The power and physicality of the image made me sense that some part of my own spirit had been present at Jordan's death—and Jordan later confirmed this.* I could feel him as heat and energy. Even though I had actually slept through the night when Jordan died, awakening the next morning without the slightest hint of loss, I now felt that a part of me had been there to greet him at the moment he left his body.

Later I had a vivid, hyper-real dream in which we sat together at the kitchen table. Jordan made it clear that it was a visit, a chance to have one of our delicious, rambling conversations. He said he wanted us to know that he was often present at that table, watching over Jude and me.

In fact, many family members and friends have reported feeling Jordan's presence in the kitchen, the center of our family life. So my dream confirmed what they already knew—that Jordan joins us when we are together, and his presence *can be felt*.

Over the next year, Jordan's messages became more specific, often answering questions that we struggled with. For example, after his death, I read a journal that he had kept during an exchange year he spent in New Zealand. A theme that frequently emerged was Jordan's struggle to be authentic. He often described the sense that he was trapped

---

*Years after, without knowing about the dream, medium Austyn Wells reported learning from Jordan that I was there. The ability to simultaneously be a soul on Earth *and* in the life between lives is discussed in later chapters of this book.

behind a mask that prevented real connection. I agonized about this privately, wondering if he had been able to resolve these painful feelings of entrapment and isolation.

Then my friend Catherine—knowing nothing about my concerns—had this dream about Jordan and me:

We were in an amphitheater. Matt was reclining on the slope, leaning on his elbows. He was crying, with tears steadily pouring from his eyes and down his cheeks. I was standing, and to my side was Jordan. Jordan stood calmly, with his legs slightly apart and his hands comfortably in his two pants pockets. He told me that Matt couldn't see him, but I could.

He told me to give Matt a message and insisted that Matt would know what it meant. He said very simply, yet with such clarity, "Tell him I went [to this life] to practice, and I didn't fight the mask . . . he'll know what it means."

I felt the message very intensely in my being. To me, it meant that he showed up to life. He knew there was a persona, but he stopped struggling with the gap between his true existence and his "mask."

I felt enormous relief. My fear that Jordan had been overwhelmed with self-disgust just disappeared. I also let go of the sense that he'd been trapped and alone in New Zealand.

I began to feel more and more hopeful that our questions, if they were clear and deeply felt, would be answered. Remarkably, Jordan continues to respond to our fears and concerns to this day.

Listening is everything. The entire community of the deceased person needs to listen. If you have lost someone, be sure to ask people to report times and situations in which they sense the presence of your loved one, including any of the following:

- Messages that come through dreams
- Unusual occurrences (for example, Jordan's older sister, Dana, had a falcon stare at her for an hour through her office window on the twenty-sixth floor of a building in Los Angeles)
- Objects associated with the loved one that suddenly "show up"

If friends and family are committed and open, the signs will come. When people are encouraged to write their dreams and feelings over time, they will create a collection of "sightings." This record of contact can then be shared with everyone, nurturing each friend and family member.

Don't worry about skeptics. Mostly they will keep a respectful silence. If they don't, ask them to accept your journey, regardless of their personal beliefs.

Jordan also provided specific messages when his

mother planned a trip to honor his memory a year following his death. Jude was about to leave for New Zealand, where she was planning to hike the Milford Sound trail. She hoped somehow to encounter Jordan there—but she feared the silence would continue.

Then Catherine had another message: "I dreamed that Jordan told me that some part of his spirit was in this beautiful, mystical, jungle-like plant. When I woke from the dream, I had a strong feeling that he was calling to his mother, that she would hear his voice calling her to him in the jungles of New Zealand."

The message was clear: Jordan would be waiting for his mother on the Milford trail. While Jude didn't consciously encounter him in New Zealand, she went to all the wild places he'd gone to, saw his friends and heard their memories, retraced his steps, and experienced *his* world without the filter of her own.

Jude has since developed a strong sense that Jordan comes to her in the form of birds—in particular hawks and hummingbirds—and she feels uniquely close to him when she sees these birds in her environment. She doesn't believe that he *is* the birds. Rather, when the birds are present, it means he is close by. Catherine's dream confirmed Jude's sense that Jordan is present in her life when she thinks of him or needs him.

Let me offer one more example. Recently I was besieged with thoughts that I was failing to love and stay connected to Jordan. After five years, the pain of loss was less, and I felt that somehow I was abandoning him—as if the pain was itself a wire holding the current of our relationship.

And then I had this dream: I was led to a library, where Jordan met me. I started to push through the doors, but he said, "Only the dead can enter this place, a sanctuary where they might review past lives and learn from mistakes." Jordan smiled at me, and suddenly I felt the full intensity of my yearning for him. I stifled a scream that kept welling in my throat. And then the message came: "This is your true feeling of loss. But it would cripple you; it would make you unable to do your work. You have ways to soften it—so you can do what you came to do."

I continue to listen. The people who love Jordan are listening. What one of us cannot hear, another one will. The record of his love holds us all, and it reminds us that the circle is unbroken. He cannot be seen, but he is present. He is in our kitchen, in our hearts. He is a thought away. And we, collectively, hold the door open.

CHAPTER 4

What Is Death?

The nun walks slowly in the aisles.
Children stare at their palms, a finger
tracing the lines. She bends from side to side.
"It stands for mortal," she says. "It is a sign
from God that you will die."
From the windows, white row houses step
down to the sea. The streets are shadowless, supine.

The ones who have not yet found it raise
their hands. She shows them the murmurs
from the bed, the last sound.
No one is afraid. Thin strips of lawn
inscribe the paths and driveways up
and down the block. A scarfed woman sweeps.

My boy tells me about death.
"They can never talk to us again," he says.
I see the mark on his palm.

I stare at it, inviting the feeling of loss.
As if death were generous, as if
death were the giver of love.

I wrote this when Jordan was six. As it turned out, Jordan and I would both discover that we could talk past death. But my sense that death can stir the deepest forms of love has turned out to be true.

I've always been aware of the closeness of death—in the presence of beauty, in joyous moments, in the fragile ways we join and lose each other. As a child I was deeply moved by tales—mostly in things I read—in which the dead influenced, or communicated with, the living. And I seemed to collect these stories, finding in them some ineffable comfort. This was long before I had any personal experience with death, and years before, as a young man, I began to fear death as the absolute end of consciousness.

As a young adult, I found that the many stories I'd heard of post-death communication occupied a place in me that lived right next to a chronic, well-nourished despair. And when, late at night, I imagined the moment of my last thought, my last awareness, I also found myself composing after-death messages I would somehow convey to everyone I loved. For all my fear of death, I somehow felt I would go on loving, holding, being with everyone who mattered.

This dialectic—a morbid terror with the competing

sense that the living and dead remained together—held me captive for years. Then, around the year 2000, I read about Michael Newton's research on the life between lives.* Newton is a psychologist. While regressing a patient to see if past-life occurrences might have a bearing on her present symptoms, he heard a startling tale. As is common, the patient described her death in a past life. But the narrative went on: she told of being met by guides, of rejoining her soul group (a family of souls who reincarnate together over many lives), doing a life review, meeting with a council of elders, and engaging in myriad learning activities with her group and her guides. Newton immediately realized this was nothing like any past-life regression he'd seen or heard of. His patient was reporting events that hadn't occurred on this planet; they belonged to a life between lives.

Over a number of years, Newton hypnotized hundreds of people, guiding them past the moment of a previous death and encouraging them to describe what happened next. Never suggesting what they'd see, Newton prompted his subjects by asking, "What is happening now?" and "Where do you go next?" Remarkably, across hundreds of naive subjects, there was near-universal agreement about the main events, processes, and locations in the life between lives.

---

*Michael Newton, *Journey of Souls* (Woodbury, MN: Llewellyn Publications, 1994).

As I read Newton's book *Journey of Souls*, I was frequently overtaken by tears. His words seemed to be describing something I had always felt, always known—even as a child. And I experienced a sense of rightness, of things falling together that had been long separated by ignorance and doubt.

Newton's subjects reported living hundreds of lives, each carefully chosen to teach lessons relevant to that soul. The purpose of living, according to these reports, is not to undergo a pass-fail test that earns a trip to heaven or hell. The point is to grow, to learn, to accumulate wisdom, for both ourselves and the evolution of all consciousness. Newton's research suggests that our life purpose—individually and for all souls—is to *become*. Embedded in this idea are important implications:

- We are in this together, and we never lose each other. The souls who reincarnate together, life after life, are like a repertory theater company. We have many parts in hundreds of plays, but the circle of love and relationship is never broken. We rejoin in the life between lives to review our work and learn from what we've done.
- The purpose of every life is both particular and universal. In particular, we choose life circumstances that will resolve karmic debts, unlearned lessons from previous lives. Often we sign up for plays that will likely bring specific kinds of challenges or pain—not for the

pain itself, but for what it teaches. Beyond the particular lessons exists the universal work of all incarnating souls: learning how to love in the face of pain and loss. We need to forget everything we know about our eternal home to learn this one, which is why we begin each new life in a state of deep amnesia.

• Everything we do—even things that cause pain to ourselves and others—is part of our, and their, learning and growth. This means that there is no sin in the way religions teach it. There are only lessons that we fail to learn or that we're slow to learn. There are only the classic mistakes (such as making our lives about seeking pleasure and avoiding pain), which we will correct sooner or later, in this life or in lives to come.

Newton's stories of the life between lives—which I read years before Jordan died—changed my cosmology. The problem was that these stories remained just words in a book—until about two years before Jordan's death, when a friend suggested I could do these regressions myself. And, further, this friend, Kim, insisted on being my first subject.

I'm a trained hypnotherapist, and over the years I have done hundreds of inductions with my patients, mostly to work with issues related to anxiety, trauma, or health. But the life-between-lives induction, as Newton does it, is a multistep process that can take four or more hours and be emotionally and energetically draining. Nonetheless, Kim and I decided to proceed.

———

We meet on a late May afternoon in my office. Kim arranges herself across carefully placed pillows on my couch. After a long muscle-relaxation process and count-down, Kim is ready to go deeper. I suggest that she is in a meadow full of golden light. I encourage her to levitate, to drift up to examine the highest trees and then skim over a stream, feeling the water brush the soles of her feet. At the end of the meadow is a stairway going backward in time. As Kim descends the steps, she stops to examine eras in her life: her room at age fifteen; a moment with her parents at age ten; the school yard at age six; being held as a toddler.

And then she is in her mother's womb. In this place she can feel her mother's emotions and her own anxious waiting for life in the world to begin. Next I suggest that Kim can see a tunnel, and when she enters the tunnel, she will pass from this life to her last one. At the end of the tunnel, Kim arrives in a field where she is hanging up wet clothes—she is a washerwoman on a plantation in the American South. This is a difficult, lonely life, where she will die young.

When I progress Kim to her death as the washer-woman she is struggling to breathe. She has consumption.

At the moment of transition, as Kim drifts above her body, she feels an enormous release—not just of physical pain, but also of the desolation of that life. She sees the plantation cook, a soul who has been with her in many incarnations, bending over the body. But by now Kim already feels a soft tugging that starts to pull her upward and away. In a few moments she arrives at the first stop on her journey home.

———

Kim went on to describe a life-between-lives experience that was like, in every important detail, those of Newton's subjects:

- She was met by a guide.
- She found her soul group (companions who had learned with her across many lives).
- She did a comprehensive review of her existence as a washerwoman, examining how she responded to pain by disconnecting from all potential sources of hurt.
- She met with her council of elders to examine key themes of this and previous lives.
- She eventually entered a process of choosing her next (this) incarnation.

Because Kim had already read Newton's book, nothing about her experience during regression provides support for his discoveries. What's meaningful about her regression to the life between lives is that it allowed her to identify her core life purpose for this time around. Kim now sees that her work is to learn how to stay open and emotionally engaged with loved ones when she is hurt, including when she is facing loss. She must also resist caving in to anger and hopelessness—a hallmark of past lives. This karmic knowledge would not have been available without the glimpse of her last incarnation and the lessons— at home with her guides, her soul group, her council of elders—that she learned during regression.

My experience with Kim deepened my conviction that the life between lives—if we can access it—is a source of vital wisdom. An opportunity to learn more came when my friend Catherine asked me to regress her.

———

It takes a forty-five-minute induction for Catherine to get deep enough to enter a past life. She arrives as a child, staring at a modest Tudor-style house. In this incarnation Catherine is male; her name is Timothy. Two sisters [also siblings in her current life] are in the courtyard. The scene appears to be nineteenth-century England.

As I progress Catherine in the life of Timothy, she describes working at a newspaper as a young man—he is an activist trying to publish the truth about events of the time. Later, he becomes a minister. In this role, he attempts to convey spiritual truths from the pulpit.

At the time of Timothy's death, he is living alone. Catherine tells me that solitude has been an essential part of this life. Aloneness provides a field for the cultivation of spiritual and emotional learning. Catherine recognizes her soul *essence* in this old man dying in his bed. She says, "His quest to find and convey the truth, his desire to seek clarity through contemplation, his core peacefulness are parts of me—my soul."

Now Catherine is drawn away from the room where Timothy died. She moves through what seem to be clouds until she emerges into a bright landscape. In the life between lives, Catherine encounters guides, her soul group, and the council of elders. She reviews the lessons of her life as Timothy, and begins to prepare for her next incarnation.

———

As with Kim's, all of Catherine's post-death experiences correspond precisely to descriptions by Newton's subjects. But that isn't important. What is significant to me is Catherine's use of the experience to clarify her life purpose *now*.

Catherine discovered from the guides that she is part of a group of souls she calls *conveyors*, whose core purpose is to share knowledge. Their work is to gather what has been learned, create a community, and provide that community with new knowledge.

Catherine explained, "I now know that my purpose (acquiring and conveying knowledge) grows directly from the core of who I am. My work is a dance: connecting to others while struggling to learn, followed by withdrawing inside to make sense of that knowledge, then connecting again and trying to convey what I've learned."

A last note about Catherine's regression concerns her struggle with doubt. Throughout much of her regression journey, Catherine questioned the authenticity of what she saw. Was she viewing an actual past life, or was she making it up? Was her soul-group encounter fabricated from things she had read, or was this a real experience in the life between lives?

There is no clear answer. The images Catherine saw exist right next to her uncertainty. Truth and doubt are inseparable. And uncertainty is the atmosphere, the medium where we live. What's undeniable is that the regression clarified Catherine's sense of self and her purpose on the planet. Whether true or conjured, what Catherine saw truly changed her.

MY OWN JOURNEYS

While I went on to facilitate a number of past-life and between-lives regressions, I remained just an observer of what seemed—from the outside—a profound experience. I heard the words, the descriptions, but I couldn't journey with those in trance to witness for myself what they saw or in any way judge its veracity. After Jordan's death, it became imperative for me to make this journey myself. So, again, I turned to psychologist Ralph Metzner, who has developed a divination process that uses images of light and heat to touch spiritual centers in the body and facilitate past-life and between-lives journeys. For me, these divinations seemed little different from hypnosis. I felt as if I were in a trance.

During my first session, I experienced a glimpse of what lies past the boundaries of this life. The journey taught me so much.

———

After a preparatory meditation, Ralph suggests that I enter into a semi-dark, cave-like tunnel. A moment later, he suggests that as I emerge I should look down at my feet. I see white, hairless ankles below a nightshirt. On my feet are fallen-down woolen stockings. "Look at yourself," Ralph says. I see then that I am an old man, with white, wispy hair and crepe-paper skin.

On my right is a single bed; to the left is a large table with stacks of leather-bound volumes. Behind me is a table with a bucket, next to a fireplace and hanging pot. Straight ahead is a pair of casement windows, though little light reaches this far into the room. Ralph encourages me to move toward the light. The street outside is narrow, with a few standing carts. Buildings are made of stone; there are no telephone wires. I notice it is sunny, and my heart leaps up as if gray skies are more typical here.

Then Ralph asks me to turn back to the room. I move toward the piles of books. Some have Latin titles; some appear to be scientific volumes. In this instant, I know I have been a bookbinder in this life, and the knowledge arrives with a certainty akin to recalling the street you lived on as a child.

More knowledge arrives—unbidden, unsought. The content of these volumes is a mystery to me. I made them with great pride, even reverence, but I have no idea what they are about. Now a sadness begins welling in my chest. I feel the emptiness of this room, this life. I begin to cry.

Ralph suggests that I move back to an earlier time in the bookbinder's life. I immediately see a small town—just a few streets adjacent to a wharf area. And I recognize the cottage where I live with my wife, Elzbeth, and our two children. It has a thatched roof, and Elzbeth is standing in the doorway, calling to a boy and girl who are playing near the docks. I recognize the girl to be my daughter in this life, Bekah. Again the knowledge arrives in the same way a memory shows up: a clear and simple sense that something is so. I recognize that this is my family, and somehow I belong here.

Ralph progresses me forward, and I move to a time when Elzbeth has died; I am raising my children alone.

I see further into that life: the children scattering, my daughter moving with a young man to a distant town, my son going to sea. They will be gone; I will not see them again.

After they leave I will ply my trade, taking comfort in the binder's art. And I will withdraw into a room where I will let go of love, where I will not be hurt again by loss, but where loss lives in every shadow.

Ralph leans closer. He asks, "Your wife in that life—who is she in this one?" Instantly I know the answer, but I don't want to say. The tears start again. The answer seems improper, as if speaking it would violate the mores that anchor me.

"Do you know?" Ralph pushes.

"Yes. But I'm afraid."

Ralph is quiet, then he says, "The truth can't hurt you."

"She is Jordan." And though it seems wrong that Jordan could be my wife, that I would know him in that way, it feels absolutely true.

Next I am progressed to the day of my death. In this narrow bed, the bookbinder struggles to breathe. Someone attends to him—a woman from the neighborhood who has brought soup. I feel the moment of detachment, the sudden lightness. And the pain that a moment ago came with every breath is gone.

I watch my body from above, moving backward toward the window. A sense of loneliness and failure wells up in me, as if this dark room is the natural outcome of my choices in this life.

I back through the window, with no sense of movement or touch. And now I am above the street, being drawn slowly up. The town grows smaller, and it eventually disappears in clouds and darkness. When I see light again, it is a garden with brilliant, surreal colors. I am met by a portly, gray-haired man whom I recognize as my brother in the life of the bookbinder, and my father in this one. I am overjoyed to see him. And there is Elzbeth, my wife.

A guide, standing a bit apart, seems taller than our little group and radiates dignity and grace. I recognize him from other times in the life between lives. In a while, I feel him encouraging us, telepathically, to begin moving. I notice that we glide; while I have legs, I don't appear to need them for walking. I am told, again telepathically, that the garden scene isn't real. It has been conjured to comfort me as I transition from a physical world.

In time I arrive at a place reserved for contemplation. Souls are quiet here, attended to by guides as they review a just-completed life. I have an odd experience of watching myself as I settle in, as if my consciousness is somehow divided.

What I experience in the life review is unbelievably difficult. I must now relive every moment of my last incarnation as a bookbinder—every thought, every feeling, every emotion. What's more, I now experience the full effect everything I did had on those around me—what they felt, how they were changed. And then, through chains of cause and effect, I see how they and others were impacted far into the future. It goes on and on, so that everything I have done is seen in this full circle. The smallest consequence of the smallest choice must be examined.

What I see now, and later in the blue-domed chamber of the council of elders, is that to avoid the pain of loss, I had let go of everyone I loved. Elzbeth was the first; I had banished her from my mind after her death. I had refused to hold the cord that connects us to everyone we love, even after they were not embodied. I had rejected my daughter because she impulsively latched on to a boy who took her far away. And when my son had gone to sea, I stopped thinking of him as well.

I see myself in that life turning inward, collapsing into small routines and pleasures, but never again reaching toward someone. Never loving. As I watch myself in the place of contemplation, I see the enormous, necessary pain required to face the truth about a life. And I am gratified that I may yet have time to change this one—because I still tend to respond to loss and disappointment in the same way: withdrawing and disconnecting.

At some point—I've no idea how long I've been in life review—I am ready to see my soul group. They are in a meadow, surrounded by tall, ancient trees. A fallen trunk, barkless and white, cuts across the grass. My brother/ father and Elzbeth/Jordan are there. I see souls from my present life: two former girlfriends; my wife, Jude; Bekah, my daughter; several dear, close friends. I am crying with relief to be with all of them again. And while I know the image of the meadow is only a comforting creation, the souls who greet me there fill me with love.

When Ralph returns me to the present moment, I feel moved, yet caught in doubt. I open my eyes. My face is streaked with tears, and I wonder about the source of this emotion.

"What did you see?" Ralph asks.

I am still crying, and I don't have words. If I could say it out loud, I might tell him I can see past the curtain. I see the fundamental truth that we are not alone, that time is an illusion, that we connect beyond death, that love is the basis of all reality.

On some deep level, we all want this to be true. And what we want to be true isn't fantasy. It isn't wish fulfillment. What we want to be true is a reflection of the deepest truth in the universe. We will always feel uncertainty, because doubt is woven into living here. However, our hope that there is a life beyond this one—and that love is never lost—is not in vain. I have gone past the curtain. There is something there.

CHAPTER 5

The Other Side: Landings, Recovery, Review

THE LAST SUNRISE ILLUMINATES THE EAST. The last day begins. Soon all plans will end; the hope for what the next day brings will end.

In the window a bird sings to no one. It is over, this life. The body's heavy burden is lifted, the last lesson learned or unlearned.

Now is the gathering of moments, of every choice. We listen to every uttered word, the truth and the deception, feeling what the words brought—whatever pain or comfort.

Now is the gathering of every touch—for violence, healing, or love.

And now, in the darkness at the end of the last day, the souls arrive who know us. They have been there in a hundred lives. Soon we begin again.

LIFE ON THE OTHER SIDE

On the other side, there is a life. It is a different life, but its purpose is the same: to learn and to love. In that other life, everything that happens serves soul development. From the moment of death to the moment we enter our next incarnation, the life between lives is about supporting each soul's spiritual growth.

I have seen—through my own journeys and what Jordan tells me in channeled writing—some of what's out there. I have a deep need to know, and Jordan structured this book, and our writing sessions, to respond to my questions about the spirit world. Much of what follows is based on his answers, which are here in hopes that they can help you with your journey. But you are also encouraged to ask your own questions—through channeled writing—of people you love who are in spirit. Let's start now at the transition to spirit life, where we leave the dark, occluded tunnel and enter the landing place.

LANDINGS

Jordan describes it to me this way:

The first things we glimpse in the life between lives are designed especially for us. The purpose of these images is comfort and support for a returning soul. Images are selected that reflect each soul's sense of peace, beauty, and the familiar. Colors and size may be altered to emphasize certain aspects of the scene, serving to calm any distress associated with the recent end of life.

In the landing place, a soul notices discontinuities between features on Earth and features in the out-of-body experience. The soul may have legs but not necessarily walk. It feels the environment emotionally but not physically. The nervous system is gone; the sensory apparatus is gone. In the life between lives, returning souls get used to "seeing" from a 360-degree perspective. Awareness is vivid and simultaneous in all directions. And they notice that voices are composed not of sound but of telepathic knowledge. The guides who supervise landings can create the sound of wind or the experience of warmth (from a conjured sun, for example), but this is done only as necessary to ease the transition.

Souls returning from other planetary experiences (there are many worlds where souls reincarnate) have totally different landing images that are aligned with expectations from their particular world and what they uniquely might respond to. Basically, the landing is choreographed to provide whatever a soul needs.

As a soul begins to settle in and accommodate itself to the landing scene, some of the physical cues are gradually phased out, and the soul is made aware that the images can be turned up or down, like stage lighting. The scene is constructed to resemble a soul's familiar world, such as Earth, but it's made of energy, not matter.

In the garden where I landed after the life of the bookbinder, I was struck after a while with the lack of sounds. I noticed still later that the initially vivid colors had begun to fade. Telepathically I was told that the images were nonphysical and ephemeral.

I ask Jordan, *Who greets us at the landing place?*

Who meets us depends on what would be most reassuring to the returning soul, what level of distress or damage has been sustained in this past life, and the soul's level of development. Guides usually oversee the landing. They may be the first greeter, or they may drift unnoticed in the background, helping to direct the process.

Souls who have sustained deep losses, who need to see someone familiar, or who have yearned for a particular loved one are likely to see that soul or those souls first. And it's also possible that members of a soul group are so eager to see the returning soul that they want to be present.

Less-advanced or damaged souls may need a lot of soothing and significant transition time with guides or masters. Souls who are prone to anxiety when facing unfamiliar circumstances may be met by loved ones, but the guides hover prominently—radiating peace and reassurance. Some souls arrive at the landing place hallucinating and need to be "talked down" in much the same way people are talked through bad LSD trips. Highly distressed or damaged souls may not be met in a landing place at all. Instead, they will go directly to a place of recovery [more on this below].

Advanced souls may also skip the landing place. On recognizing that they are discarnate, they may head directly to their soul group. These souls know the way. They've made this transition so many times, they retain a map—like migrating birds—of the landmarks pointing home. While the pathways are not physical, they are directions made from unique patterns of energy. Instead of turning left at the big tree, the soul takes a path where the energy "voltage" looks as distinct as a street sign.

I've taken several other journeys past death since that first time with Ralph. In each of them, my emotional experience on landing was relief. Fear and uncertainty fell away.

It was like a deep, relaxing breath that lifted me from the pain of the last life. In the landing place I immediately felt reassurance: *I am home; I am cared for.*

RECOVERY

I ask Jordan to tell me more about the recovery process.

Not all souls require recovery. But many do, particularly if they have had a difficult life. For those in need, the place of recovery is profoundly quiet, sheltered from telepathic noise. Souls in this place are often still suffering. Less-advanced souls may be hallucinating—without a nervous system they can create literally any image, just by thinking about it.

Souls may have unresolved emotions of fear, anger, or shame that would psychically pollute the life between lives if they didn't have the recovery stage to process them. They may also carry traumatic wounds from the previous life or memories of damage done to others bound up in a karmic debt. Some souls may not even know they are dead. Such souls struggle to hold on to physical images and story lines associated with the past life. All this must be healed in the place of recovery. These souls are soothed and bathed in energy that conveys love. It's akin to massage for sore and stressed muscles. And the process continues until the soul takes its first clean breath (parallel to a baby's first breath) and can reenter discarnate life.

Healing masters have a caseload in the place of recovery. They breathe calm into each distressed soul and adjust its energy. They give the soul—telepathically—dreamlike images suggesting that they are awakening and will soon be able to see. These masters may help the soul remember its death as they gently reguide it through the immediate post-death transition.

One recovery strategy is to induce dreams about disembodied states, which support the transition to spirit life. Another is to show—through dreams or directly—new ways to understand disturbing life events. These events, and the surging emotions they trigger, must lose their sting for a soul to "hear" and connect in the spirit world. Overwhelming emotions render a soul deaf to most telepathic communication and unable to navigate in the life between lives.

Although feelings of failure or regret can be managed in the spirit world, this is not true for rage, terror, or self-hate. Such negative emotions make the soul like a whirling dervish, ricocheting off other souls and groups, unable to connect.

The place of recovery creates acceptance for the detritus of living. We all know that living leaves scars. Our physical existence inevitably brings some damage to our soul energy, and major disruptions must be repaired by masters who know how to reweave our spiritual fabric. This work—healing and recovery—can take a few minutes or an extended period.*

LIFE REVIEW

What about life review? I ask. *Does that happen next?*

There are two kinds of review. The first happens soon after death and involves going through the Akashic Record, which is a spiritual database of every act, thought, or decision experienced by every soul across every incarnation. In particular, a review focuses on how a soul's decisions affected everyone inside the spreading ripple of cause and effect. It takes time, and there is often a great deal of empathy-based pain. Masters titrate the process so a soul doesn't get overwhelmed. They basically turn the movie of its life on and off. Then, in the space

---

*As I understand it, time in the life between lives does not correlate to Earth time, and an "extended" recovery period can feel like hours or centuries to the soul experiencing it.

between episodes, they help the soul integrate each scene into the soul's sense of self: "I did that, felt that, thought that . . . and I can see it as part of all the rest of me." During this process, masters shower souls with acceptance—framing damaging choices in the context of all the pain of living.

During review, it's important for the soul to be able to "sit" with failure—in the same way meditators sit with physical discomfort or difficult emotions. Failure is the core experience that allows for becoming and change. It isn't bad or wrong in a spiritual sense, but it must be faced. The only really wrong thing a soul can do during this review is *refuse* to face failure—through denial, hubris, blame. This extends the review or necessitates special training. Accepting failure is seeing the truth of how things really turned out, which includes seeing the actual consequences of every choice. Intentions are important, but the outcomes provide the seeds for growing wisdom.

The place where life review occurs sometimes appears to souls as a library or courthouse with a heavy classical facade. Inside there are halls with high ceilings that seem to stretch forever. While such images are common, it's also common that reviews take place in rooms where souls are spread out in what appears to be quiet study.

For me, during my regression with Ralph, the review hall looked like a meditation retreat with souls sitting in poses of deep contemplation. I wonder if I've created that image.

That's right. As with the landing place, these images are fashioned from energy, not matter. They reflect a soul's emotional attitude toward the review process and are no more "real" than the landscapes of dreams.

While some souls conjure a courthouse image for the place of review, it's likely a reflection of their own fear of the process. No actual judgment takes place. In fact, life review has nothing to do with good/bad or right/wrong judgments. It is solely about choices and outcomes: what we do and what happens after. Instead of judgment, the soul is allowed to truly *see*, which changes it at the level of soul DNA. The soul is no longer the same, and all of soul collective consciousness is no longer the same. Life review powers the evolution of soul DNA.

The second kind of review takes place during soul-group "class work." Much of it is based on hypothetical questions from guides, such as, "If you do x, what happens?" Soul groups struggle with these questions. Then they are shown "clips" from the Akashic Record of their lives and others' lives to see what actually happens when a soul does x.

Essentially, this is training in the psychology of consequences.

But there's more to this. Part of the review involves looking at the soul's frame of mind at the moment of choice, with the goal of cultivating a consciousness that has a clearer vision of outcomes. Because choices are so determined by perception, life review attends to how we arrive at our sense of what is so—and also what ends up distorting it.

We choose based on what we know, but souls have different levels of skill at seeing the truth. Consequently, learning how to separate false from authentic perceptions is part of the process of review. False perceptions are driven by desire and by efforts to hide from pain. Life review looks at how desire and pain avoidance interrupt perception—like static interference on a radio— and lead to choices based on false stories and misunderstandings.

Review is also about letting go of old rules and mores. During our time on Earth, there is often a discontinuity between the rules we live by and our ability to actually see the outcomes of our choices. What we thought was right, or convinced ourselves was right, often doesn't fit with the results of our actions.

Seeing and feeling the pain resulting from

our choices is the primary way we learn in the life between lives. The outcome of actions *is* the Akashic Record. It is the source of wisdom. It is the knowledge that we contribute to the conscious whole.

Life review is humbling because all the excuses and reasons we created for our actions dissolve. The hubris drains away, as do the lies that preserve incarnate self-esteem. Life review is where souls separate from false values and coping patterns—justified during life—that do damage.

For some, the pain of life review is more difficult to experience than death itself. It involves the transition from the untrue to the true, which brings souls from the comfort of delusional belief to the sharp clarity of what is so.

During life review, and in the soul-group classrooms, we acquire wisdom that we carry forward to the next life. But because of amnesia, we can access that wisdom only through some form of contemplation—prayer, meditation, wise mind, channeled writing, and so on.

Plato said we always choose the good (what appears best for us). But knowing the good—especially when we are pushed around by a body's unruly nervous system—is only possible by finding our way back to the wisdom gained in life review.

CHAPTER 6

Reunions

About two years before I began working on this book with Jordan, he shared the following through channeled writing.

> The current of time appears constant. We seem further from the source and more alone as one by one our loved ones leave the river.
>
> But time flows only within the banks. The villages we live in between lives are above the river, outside of time. We enter time to forget, to believe the river is all there is, cold and deep and rolling. We can enter the river anywhere—from the headwaters to the mouth. From the Stone Age to this world's end. Time receives us, takes us, teaches us—till at the end of each life we drown. Over and over.
>
> Time was invented by consciousness to measure change. We enter time to change, to grow wiser and stronger in the water. Whatever we learn is

taken back to the village, to the place where we are all becoming god.

As the progress of the book moved forward, I found myself returning to his message, hoping to gain a clearer sense of these villages outside of time.

SOUL GROUPS

I ask Jordan, *When do we get to join with all the people we love?*

When we leave time and return to the spirit world, the illusion of aloneness and loss ends. As soon as possible, we reunite with loved ones. While there is a vast network of billions of souls, we actually live in small communities.

The people in each soul group (five to twenty souls) are a family who metaphorically reside in one of the "houses" in the community. Neighbors who live in houses up and down the block and on nearby streets are often very close and support one another. And, of course, in each "town" everybody knows everybody.

Since we live in small communities, we often have many relationships—some of them long and deep—with "soul friends" outside of our immediate soul group (house/family). Sometimes we even form relationships to souls in distant groups, as we do on Earth to people in distant cities. Connections to souls in faraway groups are usually forged during incarnations, and the love may be very strong—as between soldiers from different places who forge deep bonds in war.

In the life between lives, neighbor groups often congregate in "block parties" for shared recreation, "town meetings" to explore an issue of mutual interest, or "lectures" from a master who has perspectives to offer souls at a certain point in development. Souls in the neighborhood are often at a similar spiritual level, in much the same way incarnates live in communities where everyone has a similar socioeconomic status. There's a reason for this. Across the many billions of souls, there's a huge range in level of development. Souls at various levels of consciousness see existence through the lens of different memes (assumptions, values), so we tend to congregate with those who have a similar perspective. The point is that we hang with our buddies—those with whom we share a common bond—both here and in the life between lives.

Soul groups are essentially seminars, led by guides/teachers, that go on for millennia. Much soul-group class work involves study of the Akashic

Record—parsing the intricate patterns of cause and effect as experienced by everyone involved in an event. Souls are learning to be historians, working on the eternal question "How did this happen?" The answer is in the record: including the state of mind of each soul involved in the event, the moment of each choice, and how the laws of change [which will be explored next] flow through unfolding scenarios. As souls learn about the past in their study groups, they are instantly there, witnessing. They see everything in the moment it happened.

Soul-group classes learn how to use the laws of change on Earth so they can alter cause-and-effect forces during future lives. Nelson Mandela is an example of someone who was an expert at using the laws of change on Earth. Instead of seeking revenge after years of imprisonment, he sought national reconciliation. His response was so unexpected, so anomalous, that it elevated the consciousness of many souls in South Africa and around the world. He did that by using energy patterns that interrupt habitual ways of seeing and reacting to abuse.

When a person is harmed, the usual response is to (1) get angry, (2) get power, and (3) get retribution—to harm whoever has caused the damage. Laws of change are counterforces to cause and effect. They involve souls doing and saying strategic things to alter predictable outcomes.

The more advanced a soul group is, the more advanced this training is. Souls start by learning to make small changes in the expected response (for example, raising an eyebrow instead of frowning), which will alter a single interaction. Advanced use of the laws of change can alter the course of history.

At times, life-between-lives training involves travel. Souls take archaeological tours of the past to study less-developed universes. These tours help us see where consciousness has come from, and they allow us to glimpse, at this moment, the level to which it has evolved. Such training also explores the *nature* of consciousness: what its powers are and what it can create. We study how consciousness seeks truth and how once it does, it can create laws, relationships, objects, and even a universe to reflect that truth. Our universe is mostly dark, composed of truth that is not yet seen. But as collective consciousness becomes more advanced, each succeeding universe we create becomes more light, more seen, more self-aware.

The work of souls between lives is constant learning, constant growth. Each truth that we learn—whether about our last life, the laws of change, or how consciousness evolves—brings a form of ecstasy. It is the feeling of seeing more clearly, more precisely, what is and what can be. This feeling is very similar to the feelings that we experience as embodied souls when we witness great beauty. The poet John Keats was right: seeing beauty and seeing truth produce almost the same emotion.*

While we are a part of all collective consciousness, our primary sense of belonging is to our group, soul friends, and guides. Those are the souls we long for during each incarnation. We are overjoyed at finding them—both during life and on returning to the spirit world. Conversely, the loss of these souls, through death, can trigger deep grief and aloneness.

THE SOUL GROUP ON EARTH

How does our soul group connect to us on Earth? I ask.

During our embodied life, souls from our life-between-lives neighborhood show up in various relationships and roles, including but not limited to:

- influential teachers
- nurturing grandparents

---

*"Beauty is truth, truth beauty," from John Keats, "Ode on a Grecian Urn"; available online at PoetryFoundation.org.

- siblings, parents, or children
- lovers or life partners
- friends, enemies, or foils
- colleagues or mentors
- objects of unrequited love
- lost loves
- competitors
- favorite bartenders
- doctors, therapists, advisers, violin teachers

Members of soul groups, neighboring groups, and special souls from distant groups agree to show up at a given time and place on Earth (or other planets). In advance, they sign up for roles in an ongoing series of plays, with relationships and scenarios already shaped by long chains of cause and effect. In truth, they aren't agreeing to a single drama, but to a part in a production that began years before their birth and will continue long after they've left the stage. Each relationship—with likely challenges seen in advance—is designed to provide karmic lessons.

So souls show up, like beacons during life, to guide us, to offer lessons we planned in the life between lives, and to challenge us with adversity. Souls recognize others from their group and neighboring groups, as well as soul friends, by energy—complementary vibrational patterns. This is akin to old friends making an old, familiar joke on reuniting, or a well-known voice murmuring hello. These familiar, usually recognized, energy patterns create sudden trust and a desire to connect. But they can also be dangerous. Members of our own or neighboring groups who have gone off the rails in a particular life can do enormous damage to us on Earth because we let them in without the normal caution or defenses.

While our roles in this world are largely assigned, the choices we make during each life are our own. And how these relationships play out may be nothing like what we planned during the life between lives. We may reject someone who was meant to be a life partner, fail to recognize a soul meant to be a dear friend, or alienate a child who is in our soul group. So while the roles and relationships are anticipated, the outcomes depend on us.

Each significant incarnate relationship remains a part of the soul relationship forever. The feelings, lessons, and love forged in that life cannot be extinguished by time or later incarnations.

So if two souls were father and son in one life, as you and I were, that connection becomes an indelible aspect of what the souls share?

Soul relationships can't be lost. In each life these bonds get strengthened as souls forge new roles and face new challenges. Souls who are deeply connected in the spirit world are a band of brothers and sisters who will never stop loving one another, though one may bedevil another in any given life. When souls are reunited after death and can finally see past a single existence to remember their hundreds of shared lives, all that's left is love. The hurts are gone. The disappointments are gone. Family is what matters.

Life between lives is different from the Christian notion of heaven. In traditional Christian doctrine, the afterlife is a place where souls see god as their reward for a life well spent. This communion with god allows them to download, for all eternity, his wisdom, knowledge, and grace.

And is that how it works? I ask. *Do you see god?*

Not really. In the life between lives, souls do not *see* god; they don't bathe in the light of a supreme being, or source. Instead they learn from guides and masters who are more advanced.

There's a hierarchy among souls in the life between lives, but it isn't based on worth or status. It's based instead on attained level of consciousness. At higher levels of consciousness you can do things you can't do at lower levels, such as changing the course of events in South Africa, creating living beings, or inventing new laws for a new universe. We do not see god because all of consciousness *is* god. And we are each a little part of it.

This discussion makes me wonder about other traditional concepts, like whether we are fated in this life to join soul mates.

This is a myth. Even though incarnated souls join in sexual relationships, and across lifetimes the same two souls may choose to reconnect again and again as partners, souls in a neighborhood will explore many different roles and relationships during countless incarnations. Those who've chosen to be husband and wife in one life are likely to have other life-between-lives "neighbors" with whom they've also shared a sexual relationship. Monogamy doesn't exist in the spirit world. Each relationship, each incarnated role, is entered for the purpose of learning. Rules such as fidelity—while important mores on Earth—have no bearing in the spirit world, where each soul has had countless partners from the "neighborhood."

CHOOSING THE NEXT LIFE

The last major thing we do during each sojourn in the life between lives is to choose a new life. Though we may be given several options by guides who help us decide, each path is expected to teach karmic lessons as yet unlearned in past lives. The chosen life may also provide balance. An incarnation marked by loss and helplessness may be followed by a life with greater choices. A life of extreme violence may be followed by one of relative quiescence. A life in which we have done harm may lead to a subsequent life in which we are victims.

As I think about Jordan's choice of his life with us, it exemplifies both the process of balancing and the role of a karmic lesson plan. In his previous life, Jordan told me, he had alcoholic parents, both prone to sudden bursts of violence. Throughout that childhood he lived in fear. As a young adult in that incarnation, Jordan was impulsive and restless. He became a bootlegger, using the threat of violence to control others and protect himself. Because of these activities, he lived in fear of the police. Shortly before the repeal of Prohibition, Jordan invested in a legitimate business. Things quieted down, but his life as a merchant was less successful than his whiskey-running days.

Jordan then sought balance in his next incarnation (his

life with us). Though he feared anger and had a phobia of the police, he found safety in his life with us. We observed that he took opportunities to develop competence and self-discipline, and he displayed none of the impulsiveness of his bootlegger life. He developed an appreciation for natural beauty, where he also found peace. But there remained karmic lessons and debts. Three times in his life as Jordan, he was a victim of violence—and karmic forces, unknowable to me, were at work on the night he died.

Jordan said he knew his life with us would be a short one. In our soul community, we all knew it. Though it is hard for me to believe I signed up for this—losing my boy—everything I know about the life between lives suggests we walk knowingly, deliberately, into our next life.

Jordan says:

Our last moments before incarnating can be poignant. It's hard to leave the spirit world because *everyone* is there. It is only in time that we have sadness, the illusion of separation, the apparent loss of the ones we know. Only in time do the wolves come—that image of abandonment, a lonely death— to devour us. Only in time do we know fear—the gleaming eyes of animals waiting in the dark.

Yet out there, just beyond the last breath, is everyone. We have just forgotten. It is their eyes gleaming in the dark.

CHAPTER 7

All Together:
The Living and the Dead

AT THE FUNERAL, all eyes are on the coffin. As if the one inside was the victim of misfortune, struck down by some malicious fate.

Death isn't bad luck, because there is no difference between the living and the dead. The one in the coffin is doing the same thing as the one grieving in the pew: loving and learning.

There is no difference between the living and the dead because the young have already been old, already taken a last breath, already watched planets die and galaxies collide. The one in the coffin is finished with this play. That's all. And has taken everything learned back to "the whole," back to the light.

The mourners go home. And while they grieve, the departed one is in the circle, greeting a brother from one life, or greeting a father, a daughter, a friend from others. Greeting a lover who left early, and a lover who in another play was left behind. Greeting the ones who were teachers, who were antagonists, who were protectors or protected. Greeting the one who ended a past life, who was a murderer.

The circle is always complete. We are always in it, and the funeral is an illusion. While souls actually experience no separation (just as Jordan is still with me), most human minds believe that the loss of the body is the loss of the person. And that if something cannot be seen, it isn't there.

The human mind, having amnesia for all past lives, identifies each person (soul) with a single body. And if that body/person can no longer be seen, it is assumed to be gone. Lost.

But that isn't the case. Jordan's soul is right next to me, guiding me as I write this. Souls do not leave us, and the circle does not break just because that brilliant collection of molecules called a body is put in a box.

I know this, yet still I sometimes feel alone. I ask Jordan, and he explains:

The illusion of separation is perpetuated by religious images of the afterlife—an extraordinary realm so different from our planet that its inhabitants seem unreachable and lost to us. But again, it is the human mind creating fictions.

Images of the afterlife imbued with religious

constructions of god and fantastic beings (for example, archangels and demons) are inventions of priests and holy men who attempted to make the journey while still embodied on Earth. Often aided by drugs or assaults on the body (including pain, sleeplessness, sensory overload, or deprivation), they saw in the "afterlife" what they wanted to see, what they feared seeing, or simply what their minds created in an altered state. The Tibetan and Egyptian books of the dead, the Upanishads, and the visions of countless mystics are examples of these journeys.

The Christian image of heavenly hosts singing god's praises is also just a lovely hallucination. Such images—clouds and harps and angels at the gate—create hope. But paradoxically, they place embodied souls further away from those in spirit, making it seem that discarnates are in a place that's sublime, distant, and inaccessible. These invented images hide the fact that departed souls are as much with us now as they were in life—perhaps more so, because now they are present as soon as we think of them. Telepathy covers any distance, instantly bringing souls together.

Souls in spirit love us as much as ever, think of us as much as ever, laugh with us at the absurdities of life, feel concerned about our pain, and celebrate our good choices. There is a simple reason for this. The relationship between living and departed souls is as deep, as vibrant, as committed, and as much in the present moment as ever it was on Earth.

This seems true to me. I am more in contact with Jordan now than I was at any time from when he left for college at eighteen until he was murdered at twenty-three. I consult with him often—about everything from family issues to personal choices. I send and receive messages of love and encouragement. And we are writing this book together.

I cannot hold or kiss my boy, which is a tremendous loss. But I can talk to him anytime, anywhere. There is no barrier—in this or in the spirit world—that can keep us apart.

THE STRUGGLE WITH DOUBT

The only thing now standing between us is my own doubt. The doubt visits often, whispering that my conversations with Jordan are wishes rather than truth, and that all he has taught me is a fabrication, my own thoughts attributed to him. When in doubt, I withdraw. I seek him less. I feel frightened that I'll discover something false in what he says, which will destroy my faith in us.

The doubt is unavoidable. I've learned that I must live with its whisperings even while I listen to Jordan. The doubt never leaves, because in this place absolute truth is hidden from us. Mother Teresa wrote that most of her life was spent with no sense of the presence of god. And whether or not the god she thought existed is really there, this dialectic remains: the quest for truth and the uncertainty are inescapably one experience.

Jordan says we are like shortwave radios, tuned to the frequency of some distant voice. Through the static, we pick up a phrase or two. We try to sew that into some coherence, but we have caught only a part of it. Through desire or projection, we may supply the missing words and get most of it wrong. But still we must listen.

I've learned one more thing about doubt. My need to send Jordan love and feel his love in return is bigger than doubt, bigger than the uncertainty and loneliness of living here without being able to hug my boy.

THE DUAL LIFE OF SOULS

I ask whether souls vacate the spirit world when they incarnate. Jordan responds:

> Souls who incarnate live in two places—on their chosen planet and in the spirit world. Our soul energy is divided. Souls will never take all their energy into a physical body. Some is always left behind with their soul group. As a result, every

member of a soul group is always there, in spirit, even while fully engaged in an embodied life.

Each soul has enough energy to allocate in this way, and the parts of the divided soul* communicate with each other during incarnations. This communication often takes the form of intuition, a surprising thought, a dream, a sudden impulse, or a wordless yearning.

Because soul energy is divided, and some part of us remains home in the life between lives, there is always a part of us that knows the truth. There is always a part of us that's fully aware of our purpose here. And because we live simultaneously in two worlds, there's always a part of us that accepts and understands the good and not good, the success and failure of everything we've done.

DO SOULS MERGE?

I also ask Jordan about whether our individual souls eventually merge into one oversoul or permanently join collective consciousness. He replies:

I'm still here, aren't I? I'm still talking to you. So the idea that on the point of death we all dump into some merged state can't be right.

---

*In Hindu mythology, the incarnate part is known as *jiva*, and the discarnate as *atman*.

And then I see the obvious: His identity, the soul I recognize as Jordan, hasn't disappeared. He holds the memories of our life together. He can describe lessons he learned as Jordan. And he shares with me experiences in his most recent incarnation.

Jordan isn't gone. He hasn't melted into a great sea of souls who have lost *self* and all connection to their former lives.

Jordan says this:

We remain as individual souls. Even though some beliefs, such as the Pali Buddhist tradition, hold that we dissolve and lose our identity in the afterlife, this is not the case. Instead, each individual soul does the learning by collecting karmic lessons across many lives, and it brings what it has learned to the whole.

Every choice we make as souls, whether it goes well or not, contributes to what we all, collectively, know. Everything we see clearly that was once clouded or obscure becomes a vision that all souls share. There is no end to knowledge; there is no limit to what we (at first with individual experience and then collectively) can see and understand.

We exist simultaneously in both collective and individual awareness. We know, as souls, what happened as a result of the choices we made yesterday. But we know, as members of the whole, how each choice merges with all that's known to illuminate the dark. This knowledge of outcomes can be the ordinary learning that happens during life. But knowledge from the whole is primarily gained in the life between lives.

Collective consciousness (the whole) wouldn't be able to learn without individual souls interacting and collecting data in both the physical and spirit worlds. Collective consciousness is a reservoir of knowledge and wisdom. It knows all that has happened, it has created all that exists, and it is gathering wisdom to make the next, more beautiful universe.

There are two eternal forces in consciousness. The first is the will to merge, to join. Yet that force is always balanced by a second force that individuates and separates. That's how we can be a part of collective consciousness and still remain souls with separate identities.

The drive toward merging has a purpose— to increase the "horsepower" of consciousness. Just as a boat gains more speed and power when more people are rowing, consciousness can take leaps when souls pull together during periods of collective effort.

On Earth, we experience the power of merging in limited ways (for example, in task groups, on construction projects, in dance troupes, and, often, in sexual relationships). Intense experiences of love, beauty, harmony, and creativity come from such moments of *joining*. When souls merge in the spirit world, the power of their collective wisdom can light dark corners of the universe.

On Earth and in the spirit world, we grow both from experiencing the power of joining and from making our individual choices. Consciousness has a rhythm that oscillates from an individual to a joined state, never staying exclusively in one or the other.

Death exemplifies these two forces. On one level, it seems that the person who has died has separated from the ones still living. Yet this level of separation is necessary for certain lessons to take place. As embodied people on Earth, we yearn for our departed loved ones (and vice versa), so our souls seek connection through telepathy and wordless expressions of love. This form of love—holding each other in absence—then strengthens our ability to know what is dark and invisible. In fact, when we hold each other across the divide of death, we are learning to hold the as-yet-unseen and -uncreated; the idea that has not yet taken form; the dark, untouchable corners of the universe that have yet to be imagined. In this way, death—loving what cannot be seen—prepares us for these larger tasks.

What allows us to hold each other past death—what allows you and I, Dad, to continue our conversation years after we last hugged in front of Saul's—is the same power that connects planets and molecules and families. Sometimes it's called gravity, or entanglement, or love. But at every level of consciousness, connection happens because of the alignment of vibrational patterns between objects or particles. Or souls. With soul consciousness, vibrational alignment is created by *knowing* the other. Knowing aligns energy to form connection and love.

Love is knowing—completely and without judgment. What you truly know you entrain with, stay with, yearn for. We stay connected to souls who are in spirit by remembering who they are.

Jordan reminds me:

My place is with you. We are physically separated, but always I am with you.

PATHWAYS TO CONNECTION

When I step back and ask myself how I heard those words of Jordan's, what grace gave them to me, I realize how the channel was opened.

- It started with the physical. Objects link us to the past. They are alive with the souls we love; they let us travel back and forth between here and earlier times. The objects we have in common with the dead often provide the first path to reconnection. Objects that best connect me to Jordan are his racing medals, his favorite stuffie (a rabbit named Wilzoff), and things he wrote.

- Chosen memories and places are another pathway. Specifically, this involves joining the memory of a loved one to a moment, a room, a special location. When I go back in time, I often meet Jordan on the trail to Bridal Veil Falls in Yosemite or in our kitchen. Or sometimes I find him on a deserted golf course we used to walk at night. In each place I can hug him, feeling his strong, compact body beneath my arms. And then, fully anchored in that moment, I can begin to talk to my boy.

- At the deepest level, connection rises from a meditation on a soul's essence, the signature feeling we carry of that beautiful spirit. Here we can leave behind particular moments, memories, or good or bad qualities associated with a departed loved one. We just hold them, entirely, in the heart. Love, entrainment, is knowing everything—at once and without evaluation—and holding it until the channel opens.

Right now I feel the tears and the truth of us, Jordan and me. When I ask him how best can we reach through the curtain—how we can keep death from separating us—he reminds me:

We must learn to love with a love that holds everything.

CHAPTER 8

Why Things Happen

You are pounding at the door
of Lori Wong's flat, bleeding
from the bullet in your back.
In a moment you kneel,
bend to the terrazzo step
and have the last thought
of this life.

The ones who killed you
go on, their lives closing
around a wound
that was never bound;
closing as if rage,
as if taking
could replace the blood

they lost.

The ones who hurt Jordan go on, while his days with us
slip further and further into the past. What was the plan,

the purpose, in his leaving so early, in the middle of a passionate life?

In the beginning I tried to explain that rendezvous—between Jordan and his murderers—as chance, as a random convulsion of fate where men who are prone to violence happened to cross his path. And I have imagined them as victims too, poured from families and neighborhoods that breed trauma. I have imagined them, impoverished of other opportunities, using violence as an instrument to prove themselves or meet basic needs.

I have tried to explain violence—and the moment Jordan died—as the poet W. H. Auden did: "Those to whom evil is done / Do evil in return."* But while that statement is absolutely true—as I know from my own work with trauma victims—I less and less believe it as the *reason* for losing my son. That's because the matrix of cause and effect is only the most obvious explanation for events.

If I let go of my pen, the force of gravity will make it fall. Cause and effect. If a child is raised in a brutal, treacherous environment, attachment theory predicts he or she will struggle with emotion dysregulation, as well as with aggressive or impulsive behavior. Again, this would appear to be cause and effect. However, falling pens don't

---

*From W. H. Auden, "September 1, 1939"; available online at Poets.org.

make choices. Our human ability to choose—through some degree of free will—tangles the web of cause and effect. Causes become harder to trace.

To understand why Jordan was killed I've had to go back to the question of why we are here. In fact, I've had to go even further, to the purpose of the material universe.

Jordan tells me this:

The purpose of matter—whether in the form of circling planets or the human body—is to help consciousness grow. All of physical existence serves this purpose. Consciousness creates matter and the laws of the universe. Then it manipulates and lives in physical worlds in order to learn and evolve. So every event is an opportunity for souls to grow. There is no tragedy; there is no loss. There are just events we learn from.

We select lives based on what will probably happen in that life, and what those experiences will teach. So our lesson plan determines the body, family, and environment we enter—including major relationships, challenges, and crises. But things don't always go according to plan, because of choices—our own and those of the souls around us. The possibilities at the moment when we select a life are often changed by the counterforce of free will.

The matrix of cause and effect, stretched over time, collides with hundreds of choices by dozens of nearby souls. As a result, what we signed up for may look very different thirty, forty, or fifty years into a particular life. To add to the uncertainty, lessons that go unlearned must be presented again in new circumstances. And karmic challenges that have finally been faced and surmounted will be dropped from the lesson plan, with new learning opportunities to replace them.

How much, I ask Jordan, *of the lesson plan for a life actually happens?*

The big challenges and major events usually occur. This is because the waves of probability are so strong and because they intersect from multiple sources. But events with a lower probability are often erased by decisions we make. For example, souls born in the 1920s and 1930s had an almost 100 percent probability of facing World War II. Where they lived and how the war might touch them wasn't likely to change. But choices they made responding to countless life events could change their circumstances—even to the point of altering the likely span of their lives.

In short, the big stuff is set. But as the force of

probability diminishes, our individual wills have more effect on what happens. This much is always true: whether events occur as planned or are affected by choice, the purpose of everything is to learn.

WHY WE MAY CHOOSE SHORT LIVES

Jordan and I also discuss why some souls choose short lives. His response:

There are lots of reasons souls don't stay long. For instance, they may choose to:

- briefly accompany and support another soul who'll have a longer life.
- teach a specific lesson to one or more souls.
- learn one specific lesson to complete a karmic process from another life.
- focus on developing a particular spiritual skill, such as discipline or compassion or independence, in preparation for another life when it will be needed.
- learn a particular lesson, such as helplessness, that only childhood circumstances could teach.
- experience a short reentry into the physical plane, though they now spend most of their time in spirit.

- give the briefest moment of pure love that will change surrounding lives.
- stay only a short time as a way to cope with the reluctance to reincarnate.
- have a brief excursion to Earth though they usually incarnate on other planets or planes.

As this indicates, short lives have many purposes. And in the course of world history, short lives were the norm rather than the exception. Only in recent times have we come to expect—to demand—a long life.

I learn that Jordan chose a short life to prepare for a longer one that will involve greater responsibilities. He tells me this:

I needed to recover from violence in past lives. That recovery was possible only with people who would hold me and protect me, whose love would make me safe again. And I needed to learn two key skills: (1) discipline and determination, and (2) the ability to face fear. My life as Jordan accomplished both those things.

When those lessons were learned, I could leave to do more prep work in the life between lives. My leaving also triggered many growth opportunities for the people who knew and loved Jordan. Much of that was planned.

He reminds me that I agreed to this:

> Mom was working on developing wiser responses to loss—so this was an opportunity for her. And it was a chance to supercharge your spiritual growth by learning to stay connected beyond my death. You needed to grow past the "science mind" you were prone to and reach across the curtain.

I ask if there were any lessons for Jordan in the moment or circumstances of his death. He says:

> I knew my murderer from a past-life connection. My death as Jordan was an opportunity to learn about victimization: how it feels for the one being hurt, as opposed to the perpetrator. That was work I had to do, and an opportunity arose to both exit my Jordan life and learn more about the helplessness of the victim.
>
> Now the one who took my life is learning about how violence corrupts the soul, how it makes our energy dense and frenetic, how it weakens awareness of our purpose here. Perhaps the worst thing is that violence deepens our sense of being

alone; it leaves us less and less held by love. So my death was the triggering event, and the lessons go on for the soul who murdered me.

WHY THINGS HAPPEN

Jordan says:

In the middle of our lives, it isn't important to know why things happen. If we knew why, we would see through the lesson and it might cease to be instructive. All that matters is that things happen for a reason. And beneath the ripples of cause and effect, beneath the material impact of every choice, is the driving purpose of all consciousness (and everything consciousness creates): to become.

Literally everything that happens is teaching us—from the ecstatic moments of connection to the moments of fearful pain—and we cannot stop learning from them. There is a force, much like gravity, that pulls us toward the circumstances of our next lesson. It isn't a conjuring trick, where the universe creates these events. Instead, it is an attraction, almost a yearning to be entangled in a particular kind of struggle. We unconsciously seek people, situations, and environments that offer a new version of old challenges that we haven't learned how to face, or new lessons that are integral to the plan for this life. So each event of our lives is pulled to us, and we to it, so that we may know what isn't yet known, complete what is partial, see a hidden truth that all of consciousness has waited for us to see.

CHAPTER 9

The Lessons of Uncertainty and Loss

THE SOUND OF TRUTH, like some harmony that only the wise can hear, rings out in the spiritual salons and in the clerics' quarters; it is heard from the high pulpits and after eating peyote.

But the *sound* of truth—the words and rhythms—is just a seduction. The emotion of certainty is just an emotion—no more true or false than any other. The mind says yes because the mind fears what it can't predict or explain.

The mind seeks the exquisite relief of order and linearity. It seeks the *Great One* who can finally explain our pain, our waiting in the dark. The mind is always ready to say yes because it is wired into us, into our hunger to make sense of this place.

The idea of truth deceives us. The light holds a million versions of the truth—no one of them complete or whole. Each is the partial wisdom of one moment, looking across one vista. Each is a moment of great vision and a lie, because certainty seduces, and in that certainty every other vantage place is lost.

We seek certainty because it is the antidote to fear. We seek certainty because it's the one thing impossible to find here.

But certainty is more dangerous than doubt. From conviction come razor-edged rules. Beliefs born of certainty harden and become swords of emotional violence. They cut and wound. They kill love because love—above all—accepts. It softens around each necessary flaw.

Certainty divides the world into what is true and false, rejected and embraced. It is the defense of the righteous, the self-willed. It is what war—in every form—is made of.

So this is certain: there is no certain truth here. And the certainty we think we find is often damaging; it is never the last word. It is never complete.

While doubt is painful, it is not a curse. Jordan has told me that doubt and uncertainty are necessary to our development as souls. They create a rocky field where things grow that can be found in no other place.

———

Sitting at my childhood desk once again, I meditate as I prepare to speak with Jordan. Behind the glass mask, a candle emits blue light. Outside, a susurrant breath of wind pushes through the redwoods. Finally, from some internal stillness, I ask Jordan why doubt and uncertainty are a necessary part of our life here. His answer comes in just a moment. Jordan explains:

Certainty is not a healthy state for souls—incarnate or discarnate. There is an immense amount we don't know. All learning must take place through the lens of doubt, which is why each thing we learn should be held as a mere hypothesis.

Doubt lies at the root of hope, and it is the experience of hope that makes seeking possible, that drives the quest for new knowledge and wisdom. So doubt motivates learning, the quest to enter what is unknown, the determination to turn darkness into light.

The doubt of incarnates, isolated as we are from our soul groups and guides, is especially painful. *Nothing* is certain; nothing is verifiable. We can't even know with certainty whether the physical world is an illusion of consciousness. And while I can tell you that the physical universe exists in space and time, my words can't prove that you aren't dreaming. Where can we go for the truth? There is no one to ask except gurus, who are often lost themselves and may be making things up.

Here's something important: the doubt of incarnates is crucial to the growth of all consciousness. That's because seeking, in an environment where nothing can be proved or verified, creates openness to all the infinite possibilities. We are unencumbered by *any* absolute knowledge, so we can soar to imagine endless possibilities.

Paradoxically, discarnates are limited by vast, seemingly incontrovertible knowledge, which makes it more difficult for them to imagine the dark, unseen corners of the universe. We come to Earth (and other worlds) to know nothing and to imagine everything. With no certainty, with only intuition and the scientific method to guide us, we can reach past the observable bones of the universe to think what has never yet been thought and to ask what has never yet been a question. That is the gift of living in this uncertain place.

We have used our experience of *not knowing* to seek wisdom since souls began inhabiting bodies. We have sought truth through myths and allegories, through epic stories passed down from our elders, through beauty, and through endless observations of what works and what doesn't. We have touched truth partially; we have at times sensed something enormous, just beyond the edges of thought. We have given all that we sensed and saw and imagined to collective consciousness—without any certainty of what was true or false.

That is what we do here.

Jordan, what are some of the specific lessons we receive from living with doubt?

Doubt gives the curtain that is separating the seen from the unseen the impression of impenetrability—the illusion of being some kind of barrier. Doubt—or, worse yet, the belief that death ends all relationships—*creates* the experience of profound loss. Since there is no loss, and the relationship between souls is eternal, doubt is a necessary precondition to learning the lessons that loss teaches. Some of these include the following:

- Experiencing deep aspects of love that can only be known in the absence of the beloved
- Holding the beloved in one's heart without receiving any word from the other side, without knowing if the relationship even still exists
- Experiencing aloneness, something that cannot be understood in the spirit world because there simply is no aloneness there

- Experiencing the necessary illusion of impermanence—the fear that nothing will last and everything will be lost, including our own existence—because it creates deep attention and attachment to each experience
- Navigating the fear of loss, which influences every choice and creates deep—if illusory—consequences for our choices that promote soul growth

So doubt (uncertainty) and loss are two sides of a coin. Though painful, they are also precious, a form of wealth that we spend through our entire lives in exchange for learning.

I ask Jordan, *What are the dangers that doubt brings?*

A life without certainty, without knowing anything for sure, *feels* dangerous. And pain we can't predict keeps showing up—unexpected, uncontrollable. There are no answers to the questions "Why?" and "What's next?" In this place of doubt, there is only seeking, only a *hope* that there is truth. So our work is to seek truth without ever knowing for sure we've found it, and to keep seeking while doubt, like a cold mist, goes on swirling around us.

This is the hardest thing about being incarnate. Sometimes we tire of the pain of not knowing, and we let go. At the far end of doubt is despair, a place where sometimes we create false certainties: that there is nothing beyond death, that consciousness ends, that the ones who've gone before us are lost and unreachable, that what cannot be seen doesn't exist.

Our work is to seek past the curtain and yet never really know. In the face of ceaseless pain—without knowing why or what will happen—we must learn not to give up.

What am I learning from losing you?

We will live apart now for years—I in my new life, and you in the life where I was Jordan. We have often done this. Traditionally I have left our lives together early. These are the ones you know about:

- I died young when I was your wife in that life of the bookbinder.
- I was the elder rabbi, and your mentor, in a yeshiva. [More on this later.] When I died, you felt very alone there, and tried to communicate to me—as you do now—through the curtain.

- I was an unrequited love in your life as a woman in nineteenth-century Pennsylvania.
- And, of course, my life as your son.

There have been others. In each case, my leaving has taken you into the heart of loss. You have learned to live there without being consumed or destroyed by the place. You have learned to go where it leads you—deeper into love, deeper into the light of spirit.

In some lives you have wandered in the dark rooms of loss and collapsed there. In others you have used compulsive work or addictions to endure the loss. In some lives—such as that of the old maid in Pennsylvania—you turned loss into a determination to help those in pain. And sometimes, through pain and doubt, you searched for me. In those moments you learned what you could never have known had we stayed together your entire life.

In the heart of loss you can *do* things and *know* things that are impossible in any other state. That has been your work.

Because we each have our own karma, we are each learning our own lessons. Some of mine have to do with commitment and determination—pushing through pain and obstacles to do what I set out to do. You have helped me with those

lessons in some of our shared lives, including my
life as Jordan.

*I love you, Jordan. Thank you for all you have given me,
including the chance to be your dad and to have had, these
years together, the most wonderful son.*

Now Jordan tells me things that are not for this book.
Then he says:

There is no end to the love that joins us.

CHAPTER 10

How Spirits Help Us

As I worked with Jordan to write the previous chapter, I found myself becoming more and more disengaged—not just from the project, but from my life in general. The doubts I struggled with regarding this book began to seep—in the form of a detached ennui—into nearly everything I did. Jordan saw what was happening and took action.

The first thing he did was contact me—as he has done many times—through my friend Catherine. At a little past noon on a Tuesday, the day Catherine and I often had lunch, we sat at a narrow table. The place was crowded, and we were hemmed in by voices.

"Hallelujah," a song sung at Jordan's funeral, came on the radio. I didn't hear it, but Catherine did, and she began to feel the visceral changes in her body that herald Jordan's presence: a warm rush; a tingling energy in her limbs; a drifting, dissociated feeling as she makes room for his spirit. Then she heard Jordan saying:

I'm here, I'm here.

Over and over. He was reminding me that he was present, watching over me. It was a direct response to my doubt.

But Jordan had more to say. A recent break in his murder case, with a possible identification of the shooter, had roiled me. I was afraid of finally seeing who took my boy, and I was afraid of being overtaken by anger, as had occurred so often when I was young. Through Catherine, Jordan told me to stay on the path of acceptance because that anger—as I've long known—would just imprison me.

Catherine wasn't eating. Her eyes drifted unfocused. "It's so strong," she finally said. "He's with you; that's what he wants you to know."

Catherine continued to be spacey as I drove us back to work, but I felt the beginning of something loosening, as if I might be relaxing after long preparing for a blow. When I'd lost Jordan, some part of me began waiting to lose hope as well, to be finally and unreachably alone. But today Jordan had repeated the same words I heard in Chicago:

I'm here, I'm here.

As it turned out, Jordan had more to say, but he needed a process through which he might convey some complex ideas. Two weeks after my lunch with Catherine, I met with Ralph Metzner, the psychologist who facilitated my past-life regressions.

I am uncomfortable in Ralph's new office—which is a big box in a long, motel-like building. Burning incense gives the air a dense, saturated feeling.

"I feel uncommitted," I tell Ralph, "to everything. I'm doing what I usually do, but nothing seems meaningful. It's as if I'm going through the motions. I feel disengaged, even from the work that's always meant the most to me."

Ralph waits—perhaps for me to say more. Finally, he asks if I'm trying to find out why this is happening. I nod.

"Maybe we should ask Jordan," he says, "and Catherine, too, since their souls seem to have connected."

"How do we ask Catherine?" I'm surprised at his suggestion. "She's incarnate."

"We can ask the part of her soul—*atman*—that stays in the spirit world. And with Jordan, we can do the same. They can both help us."

Ralph regresses me using images of white light to touch and activate key chakras, until I am in trance. In my earlier regression I met my soul group in a meadow, and now Ralph suggests that I will see Jordan and Catherine there. The scene takes shape. I move in and out of it as if entering and leaving a familiar room.

"You have been struggling with doubt," Ralph says. "Let them tell you why."

I see Catherine and Jordan in their embodied forms. They are leaning against a fallen log that slants into the high grass of the meadow. As soon as Ralph asks the question, I begin downloading information faster than words can form.

Catherine and Jordan both appear to be talking to me at once. The first thing I know is that my sense of meaninglessness and disconnection directly relates to this book. The problem is not just doubt—that what I learn from channeled writing could be made up—but fear. There is something about the book that scares me deeply.

Then they remind me of my past life in a yeshiva, a school for Jewish religious instruction, where as a young novice I was mentored by an old rabbi—Jordan. He befriended me, protected me, and tutored me, and I devoted myself to him. Then the old rabbi died. I was bereft and sought, through a form of meditation, to continue the relationship—much as I have with Jordan in this life. In my after-death communications with the rabbi, I was given a vastly expanded view of spirituality, the Torah, and life purpose. When I shared these insights with the learned men at the yeshiva, they were largely rejected. I continued conversations with my discarnate mentor, and I became convinced that there were terrible errors in how the Torah and other sacred texts had been interpreted.

These errors led people away from truth and spirit.

By now I was a firebrand, demanding to be heard. But the yeshiva elders, already deaf from fixed ideas, turned against me. I was shunned. And though I continued to live within the yeshiva walls, I was ridiculed as a fool who talks to the dead.

Now Jordan and Catherine allow me, for a moment, to experience the full trauma of that rejection. I feel the loss of my community, my home; and perhaps worse, I feel demeaned by the men I respected.

I see, at this moment, where Jordan and Catherine have been leading me. I am afraid the same thing will happen now. Should anyone from my science-focused community read this book, what would they think? Might they react as the yeshiva elders did? Might they have contempt for me? My fear of repeating a past-life trauma has led me to withdraw my commitment and belief from this work I do with Jordan.

And now the shutdown and disconnection are spreading to my life as a therapist, researcher, and teacher. The reason is simple: We can't pull the plug on something we deeply value without losing power to everything else. Every other thing I care about has lost some of its meaning because I am afraid of what publishing this book will do.

Now, in the meadow, I hear something else: this fear will not be going away. While it might help to know where it comes from, I will have to carry it with me as Jordan and I finish this book.

While I'm still in trance, Ralph asks what I've learned.

"It's just fear," I say. "I see it now, and it won't stop me."

———————

Over the next several weeks, my commitment returned to my work with Jordan and the other things that matter in my life. Yet though I was again fully involved, the doubts persisted: *Is this real? Have I invented my afterlife relationship to Jordan? Are all the lessons of channeled writing products of my own mind?*

Jordan wasn't finished with this issue yet. He would have one more message for me on the subject of my doubt. It would come through Catherine and a medium named Austyn Wells.

Catherine consulted Austyn with several goals in mind, one of which was to clarify her relationship to Jordan. She was hearing from him all the time, often with messages for me but increasingly with suggestions about her own spiritual path and purpose.

In this life, Jordan had known and liked Catherine. On one occasion, he had turned to her for advice. But they weren't especially close, and there wasn't much to suggest a deep soul connection. However, in channeled communications to me there was another story: Jordan said that he and Catherine had worked toward shared goals in several past lives, and they had a relationship independent from me.

Austyn did a reading for Catherine. Without knowing anything about Jordan or why Catherine was consulting her, she indicated that a young man was present who had died violently. She went on to describe Jordan, noting that he was functioning as one of Catherine's guides in this life.

The following day Catherine received an email from Austyn. "Jordan kept chatting with me all the way home," she wrote. "He has a lot to say. He told me that he is working on a book with his dad, helping him heal."

At that point, only eight people in the world knew about this book. Catherine, of course, was one of them. But she had said nothing about it to Austyn Wells, and she hadn't even been thinking about it during the reading. The odds that Austyn could guess that I was writing a book with my dead son are astronomically long. This left me with a clear message from Jordan. If he can talk to Austyn and tell her something she couldn't possibly know, then he certainly can talk to me and provide the spiritual contents of this book.

I'm here, I'm here.

Yes, you are, my son.

What I know now, which I had no sense of at the beginning of my search, is how the living and the dead support each other across the curtain. This is a fully reciprocal relationship. If we open the channel, the ones who love us on the other side will provide the support and guidance we need.

In the same way that Jordan is watching over me, your loved ones are watching over you. They see what you feel and fear and hope for. They see the path you are taking, and they often know the direction you need to go. In the same way that Jordan helps me when I'm afraid or full of doubt, the ones you love will reach out to you—in dreams or feelings or direct replies—if you ask.

The ones you love will stay with you—whispering comfort and touching your heart—to the end of your days. And then they will greet and embrace you at the portal. You will lean into them, letting them carry you across to your spirit life. And then you will begin with them again, in another play. Another chance to learn in this most difficult and beautiful place.

CHAPTER 11

What We Do When We Know Where Home Is

JORDAN TOLD ME THIS some years ago:

Each storm rolls down, washing away what holds us, what protects us. It takes away the walls and rooms of a world we counted on. As clouds obscure the sky, storms of the spirit obscure the truth, hiding the knowledge that nothing is lost—that the self is constant and never broken.

Souls suffer no lasting damage, so the idea of safety or protection is an illusion. There is nothing to be safe from; there is nothing we need to protect. It is all safe—everything we love. The storm is mere forgetting. A momentary blindness. The truth waits, eternal and untouched, until we remember it again.

KNOWING THE TRUTH

I ask Jordan, *What if we knew where home was? What if we knew we were here to learn, that this isn't where we come from?*

Our lives change when we know there is no end to things: no end to our consciousness, no end to our relationships, no end to living with purpose. If we, and our individual experience, are eternal, then all the following are true.

- Our greatest mistake is a minor event; it's simply a chance to learn.
- Pain is real, but it is not catastrophic. Pain steers us toward our purpose here. Pain cannot—in the life of an immortal soul—do lasting damage.
- There is no running out of time. Lessons not learned or missions unaccomplished in one life will be completed in another or in the life between lives.
- Since there is no loss, there is no tragedy. There is nothing we lose, do, or fail to do that can't be "reset" in another life for another chance to learn the lesson.
- Being "good" by following spiritual or religious rules isn't important. Moving through life in alignment with our purpose is important—taking

the path toward what we came here to learn and do. It's important to try and okay to fail.

- Neither seeking nor denying ourselves material things is important. Having or not having a family isn't important. Achieving or not achieving a career goal doesn't matter. These are significant only insofar as ownership, children, or a particular kind of work might be integral to our purpose.

- Death, no matter how painful the process, no matter how untimely, isn't tragic. It isn't even significant. It's just the only passage available to leave the physical plane. We only make a big deal of it because we forget we're eternal and that we'll be back with our friends.

- This is not our home. A physical environment isn't natural to us, and this planet is definitely an acquired taste. There are countless planets—most "easier" than this one—where souls learn. None of them is home, even though they become familiar and we often love them. Our home is a nonphysical place where we live together, connected by one gravitational force—love.

As we see more clearly where home is, our fear subsides. We enjoy pleasure but do not pursue it; we allow our time to be taken up with purpose and with remembering purpose as we decode the unconscious images and instructions we came here with.

When we learn what home is, the sense of tragedy and loss begins to disappear. There is nothing under the sun that can't happen again—if we need it to. Knowing what home is changes our focus. We wake up in the morning, and the day looks different. It's less about schedules and getting things done than a deep sense of what matters. As we look forward to the day, we see critical moments—from the point of view of soul purpose—that take our attention. It isn't the dentist at eleven o'clock or the four o'clock planning meeting that feels crucial. It's the first moment we'll see our daughter—or a friend in pain—and how we plan to respond.

Do you see, Dad? Everything is different, from the perspective of spirit. Problems are less important, unless they are problems between souls. Accomplishing a goal is less important, unless the goal connects to our soul work.

The day is no longer composed of peaks and valleys of anxiety based on our evaluation of what was done well or poorly. Instead, the day is about "warm spots" between souls. It's about awareness of love—wherever and however it shows up. "Did I say the right thing at the meeting?" doesn't matter. "Did I listen to another soul's pain?" Crucial.

When we know where home is, every day is built on a simple choice: to honor where love leads us or to choose the desires of the moment. The tasks of an eternal soul are values-based and purpose-based. The tasks of Earth dwellers who don't recognize their "home" in spirit are survival-based: merely getting from one day to the next, surviving threats, keeping safe, providing for every form of hunger. When we know where home is, there is no deep sadness from loss—everyone is right here. They are all watching over us. They are whispering to us our next best choice. They are holding us, witnessing, yet allowing each fall so we can learn.

We experience pain differently when we know where home is. It's just disappointment, a hope not realized. We are still aware of the gap between what *is* and how we want it to be. But in that gap is acceptance, a sense that such disappointment is inevitable. We will never escape the separation between hope and actual experience. What we say and do, how events turn out, are usually far short of what we thought possible.

The core experience, when we know where we come from, is interest, a watchful waiting for the moments when we can express purpose or show love. The core emotion is calm, a sense that we are not new and have faced this moment—or one like it—

before. Things will work out, even if events and results are completely different from what we had hoped or imagined. The inevitable pain is but a psychological scratch, one moment in the context of countless similar moments. It's an experience we will learn from.

As we learn, a sense of contentment steals over us. It is the contentment of doing our work; it is the profit a soul reaps from every experience—no matter how overwhelming or painful in the moment. The contentment comes from our core, our breath, the *in* and *out* of our life. The contentment comes from the experience of *yes: yes, I can feel this; yes, I can choose to love—no matter how much I've lost, no matter how different things are than I'd hoped.*

At my old desk, I take a deep breath. I can feel everyone I love around me—living and dead. I can feel how we remain joined. And I know that my purpose is to hold them, to give them my heart. I came here to find out how to send love across the chasm of loss, across the dark silence where no answer comes. Each time I do that, even a little bit, the contentment shows up.

Jordan continues:

When we know where home is, we see the moment of choice because we are paying attention. Our highest spiritual purpose is not to gain insight; nor is it to let go of the body or things of this world. Rather, it's to develop the *awareness* of the spiritual choices built into each moment: the choice to listen, to have compassion, to attend, to be open, to know and feel the pain, to do what connects, to say the deepest truth, to do good.

We know our desires, even when we see where home is. But now they don't stab us with hunger. We seek to avoid pain, but not at the expense of love. So we choose the good—not disguised by "moral" good, but the good we came here to do. We are souls in the midst of a life, of a particular lesson. And we are part of the whole—billions of souls doing the same thing. Learning.

Desire may come and go—beautiful in each sweet hope. Whether we find what we desire or it remains out of reach, knowing what home is quiets us, heals us, lets us live.

The pain of living comes and goes. It can't truly hurt us when we know our purpose. All we do is reach for a spiritual anchor, as I have reached for Jordan and he has reached back to me. We reach for a love that won't leave. A direction.

CHAPTER 12

The Cycle: Lessons Learned and Not Learned

AT THE BEGINNING, before any of this was written, Jordan outlined the entire book. During a session of channeled writing, he named each chapter and described its contents. It took five minutes.

As I write this, I'm sad because we are reaching the end of our work.

Jordan says:

Remember all those times I sat in the chair in your office? All those conversations? They will never end. This book is one small part of our conversation. It started lifetimes ago; it will continue after the last star goes dark. Souls who are joined in love keep talking, keep holding each other. Look at the night sky, Dad. The afterlife is so much closer than those lights. It is next to you; I am next to you.

CYCLES OF LIFE

I ask Jordan about the cycles of life, this chapter's focus. He says:

> Reincarnation and the cycle of life are something most souls do for a long time. We start, in early lives, by learning how to manage the impulses of a highly reactive body and mind. We also learn how *not* to act on emotions that drive us to do extreme things. Our bodies seek to make life about pleasure and pain—avoiding what hurts and galloping after all that feels good. A lot of early learning is *not* to trust what the body demands.
>
> In later incarnations, we grapple with desire—learning to recognize the venial desires that push us toward pleasure, the compensatory desires that drive us toward whatever relieves pain, and the consuming desires that sweep away everything that lies in their way. Consuming desires are the most destructive, and souls can spend many lives learning to tame them.
>
> In time we begin to see the most beautiful form of desire: the desire born of our purpose in being here. We learn to listen to its whispering voice. And it directs us, unerringly, toward people, places, and work that are aligned with purpose.

The development of a soul—in the arc of a single life, and over many lives—grows from choices. Events don't matter. The narrative doesn't matter. The *response* to each event is what matters. The moment of choice—the path that forks toward love or compensatory acts, toward a sense of *thou* or mere pain management—is what matters.

As we develop, each incarnation requires the soul to struggle with a key flaw (for example, addiction, shame, fear, hubris, narcissism), which, in fact, is a gift. It is the illness we have chosen, the work we have selected to do. The flaw both drives us to catastrophe and lights a path toward the learning we came here for.

Our virtues, which we celebrate and weave into our identity, are less important than the flaw. Our virtues are the toolbox we were given for the struggle. But it's the struggle itself—and the choices we make—that matters above all.

Each new life is a return to school. The pain is nothing—momentary if you remember why we're here. When you look at a sunset, it is a beautiful end: a day that is over, where every choice has been made and cannot be made again. Death is the same: the choices of that life have been made and cannot be made again. And yet . . . on the next day, or in the next life, they *can* be made again. That is the cycle—learning on the next day what was bollixed on the day before, discovering in the next life a choice that eluded us in the life before.

There is no end to the time allotted for learning. Each of us—and all consciousness—will keep learning for all eternity.

Religions use the word *eternity* to mean an endless state of either reward (as in eternal reward, eternal rest) or damnation. But there is no eternal rest, no eternal reward. There is just an eternity of learning. Growing. Seeing new things.

I ask Jordan, *Why are we doing this, learning forever?*

The universe, all of consciousness, needs us to do this. We are each here to do something that *only we can do* and that needs to be done. We are here to learn something—different from what every other soul is learning—that all of consciousness needs to know.

No one else can learn—in quite the same way— this lesson; no one else will discover this precise truth or the wise course each of us must find. So the lessons *must* keep showing up until we find a new response.

KARMA

I ask Jordan, *Is there any difference between karma and learning?*

> Karma is essentially the *momentum of learning.* The lesson presents itself, over and over, until our choices change. It continues until we abandon the old, habitual response for something new. The lesson must continue—karma requires it—until we have sought and made a wiser choice.
>
> Suppose you have, over the years, tended to withdraw from people in pain. You're protecting yourself from their torment, but at the same time you're abandoning sister and brother souls. You are breaking these connections; you are failing to learn how to love in the face of pain. The momentum of your learning—karma—will keep bringing these same, needy people across your path. You will be a magnet for them until you find a response that includes love.

Jordan is reminding me of a dear friend—Mary—whose desire to help others has been tempered by their overwhelming needs and pain. Mary has learned to "give them my fingertips." By this she means that she extends her love to them but does not let them grab and pull her under.

Mary has learned to hold a loving connection without letting herself be consumed by another's pain.

Jordan says:

> As old karmic lessons are completed, new challenges will show up or even present themselves before the old lesson is learned. We are often working on more than one core lesson in a life. Just as some lives have more pain than others, some may also have more karmic challenges. This isn't a sign of failure or of a stubborn soul who isn't learning. The exact opposite may be the case. Often, lives with multiple challenges indicate that a soul has chosen a body and environment that will provide great and rapid learning.
>
> We don't careen from one life to another without pause. We need the life between lives to review and digest what we've done. We need to review the tape of the Akashic Record to see every choice, every word spoken, and what it wrought. It's during this review process that lessons become clearer, choices are finally understood, and the damage we may have done can finally be faced.
>
> So the cycle is absolutely necessary—from embodied life, to review in the spirit world, to a new incarnation—in order to gather wisdom and see deeper into the truth.

WHEN THE CYCLE ENDS

Jordan explains:

At some point the cycle ends. A soul has learned as much as the physical worlds can teach. There is a feeling of satiety, a sense that the physical realms of beauty and pain have been visited enough. The soul is no longer attracted to the waiting body. It no longer wants a part in the play.

And now the soul turns more completely to service—as a guide, healer, or creator in the world of spirit. It has new tasks, new things to learn. And in a rhythmic merging and unmerging with the whole, each spirit absorbs the truth of god, the truth all consciousness has gathered. The fruit of all our lives becomes the *substance* of consciousness, the light of the universe, the wisdom that breaks the barriers to everything as yet unknown.

———

I ask Jordan, *What do we do with everything we learn? What does it mean to light the universe?* Somehow this seems beautiful but insubstantial to me. Just words.

But Jordan is very clear. He says:

We learn in order to:

- love more deeply and completely;
- find more light, truth;
- and create the next universe.

Initially, this doesn't seem any clearer or more specific to me. I ask for more details, and he talks about love:

We are all working to expand the meaning of love. Love is the energy that supports the spirit world and the life between lives. But *there* it is pure, untouched by pain or loss. The experience of pure love, the golden light that awaits souls at the threshold beyond death, is beautiful but not enough. It is love without cost, without disappointment, without hunger. It is love without the *struggle* to see and know, without, to use Rumi's metaphor, the wound that lets in light.* So we incarnate to know a love that's held at great price, a love of the heart and the breath, a love of reaching arms rather than telepathy.

My love for you, Dad, is expressed by telepathy. But when you send love back, it's the *image* of hugging me, feeling my head against your cheek. And that is exactly the difference between love

---

*Jalal Al-din Rumi, "No Room for Form," in *The Essential Rumi*, trans. Coleman Barks (New York: HarperCollins, 1995), 142.

expressed in the spirit world and love expressed on Earth. The former is open, direct, and effortless. The love on Earth requires intention and choice. And the choice to love often brings pain—as your love for me must always be marbled with sadness and missing.

So love is a bigger challenge for incarnates, and in some ways it is more beautiful. In the cycle of life and the life between lives, love is constantly redefined by the presence or absence of pain. The cycle also deepens our capacity to see and know one another.

The light of the universe is conscious seeing and learning—which is the foundation of love. And the dark in the universe is what we have yet to know and love. As each succeeding universe grows more luminous, souls grow more luminous—with new love and knowledge.

In this way, the universe is nothing more than knowledge (truth) that *generates* love. It is nothing more than conscious thought.

Truth is an infinite wellspring that can never be completely known by the whole (meaning collective consciousness or god). Each of us gathers small particles of the truth in each life. These particles, which are eventually held by all souls and all consciousness, populate the universe—and each new, more perfect universe. Our work, the work of all consciousness, is never done. We go on gathering truth and wisdom across countless cycles, across the millennia on this planet and others.

But learning is not all that we do, not the only function of consciousness. Consciousness also creates. We incarnate to create new forms of beauty and truth. New thoughts and images.

In fact, everything we learn creates. Everything we learn makes something new. If you and I are talking, Dad, and you discover something, you will make a new experience from that. What you create could be a new sweetness in your relationship to Mom, a new poem, a new therapy method for your clients. And those new thoughts—yours, mine, and every reincarnating soul's—allow collective consciousness to make new things. New natural laws, a new physics, new forms of love, new ways to enter and know one another, new ways to heal, new forms of humor. Do you see? Everything we do, in every life, teaches us—individually and as a whole—something that in turn powers more beautiful creations. It is an endless cycle of choosing, learning, and making.

And when this life is over, when you return to me in the spirit world, we'll show each other what we've learned. We'll hold it so it will never be lost.

Then we'll go out again to take our parts in a new play, with new lessons.

Dad, here is what you've learned in this life: I will never leave your side; nothing can separate our souls. You can still hold me, as you did at Saul's. We will keep talking forever. We will learn from each other forever. Long after we have stopped coming to this planet, we will be making things together. This book and the long, beautiful conversations we've had in this life are a moment, a bead in the endless string threaded by love.

CHAPTER 13

Another Journey

LEAVING THE STERILE TOWERS of the Bonaventure Hotel in Los Angeles, Jude and I are driving north. Midmorning light scrapes the barren outcroppings of the San Gabriel Range. Strings of houses terrace the mountains' base. We are heading toward the home of Austyn Wells, a medium who already knows Jordan (from working with Catherine) and whose specialty is teaching people how to forge their own contact with the dead.

Arriving at Austyn's home, as we climb from the car I am struck by how different we feel now compared to that day in Chicago five years ago, when we first sought Jordan. Jude, in the intervening time and because of the experiences and messages from Jordan documented in these chapters, has gone "from hope to certainty" that Jordan is still with us. And I have been given this book, full of Jordan's voice and one core truth: that we are together, and no one we love is ever lost. Jude and I look at the trees, the flowers; we listen to the birdsong. We are, as we walk into the courtyard of Austyn's house, unafraid.

Austyn greets us in a flowing black dress. Her hair is up, framing tanned skin and an array of elegant jewelry. Her face is well cared for in middle age, and her appearance suggests both the accoutrement of privilege and a caring accessibility.

The room where Austyn works is dark, with crystals and candles and soft New Age organ music. I am put off by the mystical bric-a-brac, but I push myself to begin: "Jordan sent us to you."

Austyn allows silence. She opens her notepad and reports that Jordan is in the room. "He's excited," she says. "He's sitting right between you."

I look at the small space between Jude and me on the leather love seat, and I imagine Jordan squeezing between us. Somehow he still seems remote, a figure held aloft by ones who make their living conjuring the dead.

"Jordan says your book is almost finished—twelve chapters." Austyn pauses. "He's showing me the first four chapters, how you wrote the story of making contact with him. And then it takes off—mostly written by Jordan— explaining how life and death work." She looks at us. "Is that right?"

"That's the way we did it," I say. "Jordan told me that the last chapter would require seeking knowledge from someone else. That Jude and I would have to travel somewhere. Finally, he suggested seeing you."

Austyn concentrates, looking at me. "Jordan says everything changed for you after he died. You were devoted to science, to research, and then you . . . discovered the spiritual side. And it caused a schism in you, where you now feel less involved with science. Jordan says you have to bring these two sides together"—she knits her fingers—"so you can hold them both. That's what the last chapter has to be about—bringing the scientific and spiritual together."

This is something that has never occurred to me. And I have the thought that it's too radically different from anything Jordan and I have talked about to ever have entered our conversation. Though in life Jordan was very interested in science, since his death we have focused exclusively on spiritual questions.

Now, quite suddenly, I am downloading an entire model of how science and spirituality can interface. It shows up as both an image and an idea, at once whole and complex. I have experienced this phenomenon before— with Jordan and in communications from my council of elders in the life between lives. The entire concept arrives instantaneously, in one piece and without words. It's like a picture that I glance at and put away for later; I'll look at it again in detail when we get home.

Austyn stares down for a moment; she appears to be listening. "Jude?" Another interval passes; Austyn looks abstracted. "You have been waiting to hear from Jordan, but your medium isn't words. He can't reach you with words. Your medium is touch, sensation. That's how you can feel his presence."

Immediately I think of Chicago, where I heard Jordan's voice but Jude did not. And I recognize the truth of what Austyn says: Jude was a dancer, and now she sculpts. She *knows* things in her body and her hands.

"Jude, just let your eyes close for a moment." Austyn's voice has become stronger, less the tone of a medium than of a teacher. "Go inside and let yourself be aware of your body. In a moment, invite Jordan in; let him be present inside you. Just let him in now and feel his energy . . . what do you notice?"

"I feel a strong tingling," Jude says, "in my chest and arms."

"Okay. In a moment, Jordan will briefly move away." She waits. "What do you feel now?"

"It's gone."

"Okay. Invite him back."

For the next few minutes, Austyn guides Jude to watch as Jordan's energy enters and leaves her body. During this process, the location and physical signature of his energy become more and more clear.

"Okay, let's establish some basic communication so you can ask him questions. Have Jordan show you his 'yes' energy; invite him to show you what 'yes' feels like."

"The same tingling," Jude says, "but just in my chest."

"And now Jordan's 'no' energy. Invite him to help you feel that."

Jude waits. "In the back of my head. Tingling, but centered here." She brushes the hair above her neck.

Austyn has Jude practice "yes" and "no" and observe the difference energetically. As Jude reliably feels the shift, I realize she has found what she sought so long ago: a way to feel our boy again, to know he is with her. And more: to ask him questions and feel answers.

I experience an immense exhaustion as we embrace Austyn and say goodbye. Soft October light washes the streets and rooftops of Altadena below. We are only four hundred miles from home, and we have been gone just a few days. But I feel as if it has been years, and we have traveled past the last outposts of the world we knew.

———

After that visit, I am anxious to learn more about the intersection of science and spirituality. I ask Jordan, who says this:

Our book is our story, how we found each other through the curtain. Some may see it as just that—a story: well meaning, perhaps, yet unverifiable.

But, Dad, this is more than a story; it's also scientific data. It's not the kind of science where we measure distances to the stars, and it's not based on randomized, controlled trials. Instead, it is the science of *multiple, independent observations of phenomena*. These include:

- the thousands of people who report seeing deceased loved ones in the hours before death.
- the hundreds of children who have reported verifiable past lives.
- the countless reports of near-death and out-of-body experiences.
- remote viewing, in which people can accurately describe places they've never been.
- the hundreds of naive subjects who, during hypnosis, have reported similar life-between-lives experiences.

These are all examples of collecting independent data from many individuals; over time the sheer numbers begin to point to something.

Science and spirituality belong together. The problem is that many spiritual practitioners have rejected science, and few are demanding that science take on spiritual questions. Meanwhile, science has been hijacked by the scientific method and the obsession with measurement.

We can't measure a thought, but it nonetheless exists and can be "observed" via subjective descriptions. We can't measure the experiences of the eighty-one veterans who heard the voices of the dead through their work with Allan Botkin, but their independent, unprompted experiences should be considered real data.

I ask Jordan how we join science and spirituality. He tells me the following:

There are two parts to spirituality: the method and the cosmology; the practice and the belief. Every spiritual method, and every belief, can be examined.

Does meditation work? We already know that meditation works via dozens of studies. Does prayer work? We also know that prayer can heal and access deep wisdom. They are both paths to wise mind, to knowledge locked in the immortal soul. There are many other spiritual methods that could and should be tested as well.

If spiritual practitioners were committed to science, they would ask these questions. Consider, Dad, the impact on your own life of talking to me. That could be measured. For example, by reduced fear of death, clarity of life purpose, well-being, quality of relationships, and so on. Every spiritual practice has outcomes, and we could measure whether they are better or worse than those of other practices, or than the human baseline.

Cosmologies can also be tested. Does hell exist? Are there bardos where souls are imprisoned to atone for sins? Not one medium has found such a place. Multiple independent reports of the afterlife offer little support for damnation. A science that uses independent observations of experience could help us put the idea of hell to rest.

Science is the path to bring religion into alignment with the deepest truth. Religion that rejects science or the investigation of its methods or cosmology is dangerous. It is ripe for manipulation.

In the history of the world, people have held thousands of belief systems. These theologies were mostly far from true. But the methods, the found pathways to wise mind, were often brilliant. We have to separate path from belief, the doorways we find from mere dogma. The beliefs often spring from the fevered imaginations of priests and sages. But there are hundreds of paths to truth, to knowledge, to love.

At that moment, I have a feeling of completeness, that the book is almost finished. I ask Jordan to identify the most important thing to say at the end.

There is no end; the conversation goes on. Between

you and me. And between all the souls who love each other, living and dead.

I wait, but that is all: the simple truth that we go on—loving each other forever.

———

Spirituality is about seeking truth. It's about recognizing the markers of what is false versus what is aligned with love. This book, these conversations with Jordan, is science-based. While it is true that my experiences of after-death communication can't be measured because they are subjective and exist inside my mind, it's also true that they comprise a *single, independent observation* of the phenomenon of after-death communication. And when combined with other reports from people who have conversations with the dead, they provide *multiple* independent observations of this experience. I encourage you to compare these accounts and see where they agree—and perhaps point to truth.

You have read this because you're seeking truth. Jordan and I encourage you to be skeptical, to seek many independent observations of the afterlife. Spiritual truth is not the province of gurus, priests, or mediums. It is something to be found in the experiences of others and in your heart. Be your own scientist.

What Happens at the End of Life

JORDAN DIED IN 2008. Nearly a year later, when I learned to channel, we began the conversations that go on to this day. The book you hold chronicles my search for Jordan in that first year after his death and excerpts many of his channeled messages over the next five. But the conversations continued, hundreds of them, where Jordan revealed more than I could ever have imagined about the afterlife, the nature of the universe, what love is, why souls incarnate, and so much more.

Recently (starting around June 2024), Jordan began describing the end-of-life experience and how death is nothing to be feared—just a step in our becoming. I received the following ten channeled messages over the next six months, and they are published here for the first time. May they bring you hope and peace.

AT THE END OF THE ROAD

At the end of every long road, every life, is love. No matter what we do or don't do, no matter the pain we inflict, no matter all the choices sprung from ego and desire, love is always, inescapably at the end of the road.

The reason is this: love made the road, love drops us into each selective life, love awaits us when we finally get home, love attaches us to everything that is.

WHY WE COME HERE

In the spirit world love just *is*. It surrounds and holds every soul. It is the basis of all communication. Souls don't need to generate love because they just *have* it. So love in the spirit world is unearned, uncreated. Until souls begin to incarnate on physical worlds they will lack the ability to *create* love, to make the decision to love in the face of every obstacle, every kind of pain.

Love in the physical universe must be earned. We choose to act on love, or not. We choose to bring love into each relationship, or not. We choose to *be* love, or not. It is the *choice* to love or not that teaches us the most. And that choice, unavailable in spirit, is why we come here.

PAIN IS THE GREAT TEACHER

Pain arises—physical, emotional—unwelcome as it pierces our awareness. Since pain is unavoidable, since it keeps showing up, there's no point in plotting to get rid of it. It will show up again and again at every age and era of life.

The most important question is what do we do in the face of pain? How do we respond to it? How do we live with purpose and meaning while pain screams inside of us?

We can obsess about the means to stop it—often impossible. We can rage at the injustice of our suffering, blaming ourselves or others for the pain. We can try to punish whoever seems to be the source of our pain. We can try to numb the pain, but in doing so we'll crush our own vitality.

What if our pain exists for a reason? What if it has a vital role in life on this planet? What if it can't be avoided because pain is our great teacher, because pain exists to help us evolve and grow?

Our response to pain is the centerpiece of our existence. Do we respond with anger, numbness, avoidance, or with love? When pain comes, that is always the choice: to connect more deeply, love more deeply, or shut down and run.

THERE IS ALWAYS A FUTURE

You always have a future. And one that is endless for your soul. At the end of each life a new future opens—experiencing love and relationship to our soul families, learning with them, enjoying countless experiences of merging and knowing. Then there is our spirit world curriculum—the plan for growth and the spiritual career for our particular soul.

And finally, there is rebirth, with its own particular future, its own learning agenda.

Each particular life has a future *after death* where we can keep revisiting it in the Akashic Record and learning from every significant moment. We can also learn alternative outcomes—if we'd chosen a path not actually taken.

It's like being in a school. But a school in which we learn and grow *while* doing and accomplishing real things. Building real skills with which to love and support souls—both in the physical and spirit worlds.

So there's always a future. Death opens rather than closes it off. Death is just going home after a long field trip, a long internship to the planet.

Feeling the connection to All is one way to experience a boundless future. Love opens the door to a now stretching past the vanishing point.

Past the fear of nonexistence. There will always be a now. For each of us. Forever.

THE APPROACH OF DEATH

At the end of life we often welcome the shutting down. We have done enough for this life. As the brain drifts, the bond between body and soul loosens. The soul often moves in and out of the body as coma approaches or deepens. Consciousness flickers as the soul leaves and returns. The soul is getting ready to be weightless, unbounded. There's a sense now of being accompanied by an unseen force. During intervals when the soul leaves there is a growing feeling of being held and eventually being guided to let go.

The body's struggle to live seems less important. Even unnecessary. The body has served as long as it could; soon its molecules will begin to disperse as fluids or a last breath. This moment—the approaching goodbye—is different depending on the soul's relationship to the body. There may be loss, sadness, regret—or the sense of leaving a partner with whom we've done much. Or just a simple sigh of letting go.

This moment doesn't usually last long, except in sudden death where there was no time to prepare. But it can be the intense last vestige of an incarnation. Our residency in this body, this life, is over, and we slip out of the physical constraints for the last time. The good and difficult emotions of release pass. We wait. But with a sense that love is nearby or just ahead. A sense that there is somewhere we now belong and the beginning of movement toward that yet-unseen place.

TIME AND DEATH

Time is up. We say that at the end of an exam or a life. But time has almost nothing to do with death because our consciousness is eternal and we will forever go on learning and changing. So time only coincides with physical death when death is marked at a certain minute, hour, date, and year. Time goes on forever because consciousness will keep evolving— one moment different from the last—eternally.

The dates of a life merely mark a single incarnation. They mean nothing. The gravestone eventually leans, falls; the urn of ashes is moved and finally lost; the molecules of this body become dispersed. Nothing is really lost; merely changed. A state of constant *becoming*.

Each new thought is a part of the becoming. Each new universe—a material form rising to visibility at the direction of All, particles pouring out from the energy matrix—is part of the becoming.

Time is never up because the becoming never ends.

THE MOMENT OF CHANGE

Darkness comes and goes. Physical objects change, dissolve, reform. Your body is not lost; it continues in other forms, as part of something else. Your spirit incarnates in other forms, some of them strange and alien on other planets, consciousness evolves and grows with each new experience, each new life.

Everything changes and reforms, becomes in some way new. At the moment of change—whether it's death or loss of function or transformation into a new shape or form—there is darkness, a cessation, a pausing. The darkness can be cataclysmic or no more dramatic than a peaceful last breath.

The darkness is merely a transition. The moment between what something (including a soul) was and what it becomes. Consciousness reforms with every new experience. And in the darkness of the center of each moment of change is the infinite possibility and promise of what can now evolve.

We fear the darkness of change and transition because we cannot see beyond it, beyond the form as it exists. The new form, hidden in a future beyond words, beyond thought, awaits discovery. We have no choice except to see it and be it. But most important to love it.

There is a sense of urgency as change approaches. Often a sense of fear. It seems as if the loss of the familiar form will somehow damage us. Take us with it into oblivion. Death—as a change in form—is the greatest delusion. All that changes is a sudden expansion of awareness, a welling sense of love. A remembering of all we knew that was set aside for entry into one particular life.

Time continues to mark each change in form, each expansion of consciousness.

DEATH AS A MOMENT OF CHOICE

Death is a moment of choice—we can bring love to that moment or not. As death approaches, love can be sent in two directions—toward those still embodied who have journeyed with us and toward those we love who wait for us on the other side. Love can be spoken or sent telepathically.

When we choose love at the moment of death, fear dissolves. Embodied life, death, and life in spirit are all about one thing. And when we are that one thing—love—life, death, and afterlife roll together into a single, unbroken experience: the eternal conscious life of a soul. There is nothing to fear because nothing is lost. Everything is joined by love. Forever.

AT DEATH WE BECOME WHOLE

What have we lost in this life? We lose, while we are here, all our memories, our knowledge of past lives, our sense of growth and evolving. We lose awareness of the love that connects us to all the souls we've known beyond this particular incarnation. We forget how unimportant loss is. How everything we think is gone is merely a thought away.

Shortly after death all we thought was lost is returned to us. Every memory, everything learned, everything we cared about, all of it is given back to us. We become whole. Death is about becoming whole.

Three things happen when we cross over. We recover everything we ever learned. We connect to every soul we ever loved. And perhaps most important—we remember we are one with everything.

THE DOORWAY

We see death as the dark door—the end of light, of standing beneath the sun. But death is the door to a more brilliant light than any burning star. It is the light of love that we see only dimly in a physical world. It is the light of belonging, of feeling one. Death is graduation from the long, painful school of each life, a throwing our hats in the air. And then walking off stage to the arms of every soul we love.

ABOUT THE AUTHOR

 MATTHEW MCKAY is a clinical psychologist and a professor at the Wright Institute in Berkeley, California. He is founder of the Berkeley Cognitive Behavior Therapy Clinic and codirector of Bay Area Trauma Recovery Clinic, which provides low-fee services for people with PTSD. Author or coauthor of more than forty professional and self-help psychology books, his spiritual books include *The Luminous Landscape of the Afterlife, Love in the Time of Impermanence, Lessons from the Afterlife,* and *Why?* McKay is the cofounder and director of product development at New Harbinger Publications.

For more, visit **SeekingJordan.com**